It's time for a fresh approach to Teen Wicca, especially one written by someone who began to walk the Old Path as a teen, and now can look back on that experience as an adult. Young Wiccans will learn the fundamental tenets of Wiccan practice, guidance for rituals, and the full text of a self-dedication for those who wish to journey further. No longer should any teen Wiccan feel alone.
Edain McCoy, author of *The Witch's Coven* and *The Witch's Moon*

David Salisbury's take on Wicca is hip, slick and down to earth, and eminently suitable for the newbie. Seekers can feel secure in Salisbury's expertise as well as his fresh approach, and I look forward to recommending it to young people who pass my way, looking for an introductory text that speaks directly to them.
Ann-Marie Gallagher, author of *The Spells Bible*

In *Teen Spirit Wicca*, David Salisbury distills Wiccan practice down to its most basic elements, providing an approachable and encouraging introduction to young seekers. Most of the spells and rituals require no more than two or three common household items; this is a practice that any kid can begin in his or her own bedroom. Having started his practice on his own at the age of 12, Salisbury also speaks from experience on an issue of concern to Wiccan/Pagan kids: how to cope with bullies with both magickal and mundane methods. This is an excellent beginner's book, and I'm going to give a copy to my own 12-year-old daughter.
Jennifer Hunter, author of *21st Century Wicca: A Young Witch's Guide to Living the Magical Life*

An interesting examination of Wicca from a teen viewpoint from a Wiccan who started down this Pagan spiritual path as a teen (as I did). *Teen Spirit Wicca* is a book which will give you a useful foundation for a lifetime of practice.

Kerr Cuhulain, Wiccan author and the Preceptor General of the Order of Scáthach

David Salisbury offers keen insight for teenagers wondering where to start and how to practice Wicca. I especially like his analysis of the Charge of the Goddess, one of my favorite pieces of pagan poetry—and one that is not well understood. Being a 20-something himself, and not so far from his own school days, the author has good advice on bullying, ethics, working around being a magical kid under someone else's roof, and how to keep your balance in the middle of teenage energy. Better yet, he provides rituals, charms and spells for your own practice that answer your questions rather than leaving you scratching your head asking "Now what?" When you read *Teen Spirit Wicca*, you will know the what and how of Wicca.

Dorothy Louise Abrams, co-founder of the Web PATH Center in Lyons, NY and author of *Identity and the Quartered Circle: Studies in Applied Wicca*

Teen Spirit Wicca

Teen Spirit
Wicca

David Salisbury

Winchester, UK
Washington, USA

First published by Soul Rocks Books, 2014
Soul Rocks Books is an imprint of John Hunt Publishing Ltd., Laurel House, Station Approach,
Alresford, Hants, SO24 9JH, UK
office1@jhpbooks.net
www.johnhuntpublishing.com
www.soulrocks-books.com

For distributor details and how to order please visit the 'Ordering' section on our website.

Text copyright: David Salisbury 2013

ISBN: 978 1 78279 059 4

A CIP catalogue record for this book is available from the British Library.

Design: Stuart Davies
www.stuartdaviesart.com

Printed in the USA by Edwards Brothers Malloy

We operate a distinctive and ethical publishing philosophy in all
areas of our business, from our global network of authors to
production and worldwide distribution.

This book is dedicated to Tempest Kayne Smith (1988-2001)
and to all victims of bullying.
Stand strong and stay here with us. It gets better.

Introduction

Wicca today is a lot different than it was when I was a teenager, which at the time of writing was only eight years ago. When I started practicing Wicca in the late 90s, it was towards the end of what some might call the "heyday" of the popularization of all things edgy and occult. Black was the norm for kids who refused to fit in with the preppy masses, *Buffy the Vampire Slayer* was on primetime, and books on Wicca and Paganism were getting churned out like hotcakes. Between *The Craft*, *Practical Magic*, and the premiere of *Charmed*, the media was loving the witch craze. My magic-loving pre-teen brain soaked up every minute of it.

A lot of the grown-up Wiccans I knew at that time didn't think the supernatural craze as so cool though. They worried about having a new generation of Wiccans grow up with watered-down information and a shallow understanding of the mysteries of the Wiccan religion. I learned early on to not mention the "fun" parts of Wicca around other Wiccans if I wanted to be taken seriously. And, man, did I want to be taken seriously! But you know what happened? Instead, a whole generation (my generation) of twentysomethings started popping up with a crazy amount of information. Information that was more widely accessible to them than any generation before. The teens ten years ago are now taking on amazing leadership positions and changing the face of how Wiccans interact with society today. Pretty cool, huh?

My first exposure to Wicca was through a classmate at the very start of my 7th grade. Part of her family was Romani, which means they were gypsies. She knew all kinds of interesting esoteric things, including a bit about Wicca and witchcraft. Instead of holding my hand through the learning process, she pointed me to the bookstore and recommended some reading material. Once I got there, I picked up a copy of *Wicca* by the legendary Scott Cunningham. Luckily for me, the big-chain bookstores were putting out so many new books on the Craft, I always had something great to read. I would save up my lunch money for weeks on end just to buy a new book from the "new age" section of Borders. When I couldn't buy new books, I was at the library pouring through volumes of mythology and folklore from all over the world. The best part of all that was being able to retain so much information that I can still recall today. A young brain can remember way more information than an older one can.

My point is – there's never been a better time for teens to get involved in Wicca. You have school, friends, family, and a whole future to worry about. Learning a spiritual practice like Wicca is a great way to level out the stressors and bring some peace into the calamity of it all. Being a nature-based religion, Wicca doesn't look to separate you from the world, but rather its goal is to help you become part of it. It won't make your life perfect, but it can smooth out the bumps along the way. And best of all, it can bring some much-needed empowerment at a time when you need it the most.

Although we've made a lot of progress, Wicca is still pretty misunderstood in a lot of areas. Talking about the meaning of Wicca usually means talking about the meaning of witchcraft, which is still a pretty loaded word. In fact, Wicca can challenge us to talk about a few things that not a lot of people like to confront. Along with the glamor of magick and self-empowerment comes the work of facing our fears, setting high goals, and claiming responsibility for our lives and our role in the universe.

Sure it means we have to commit to doing some work to hone our Craft, but the whole process can still be pretty fun too. After all, if you're not interested in learning something, it's unlikely you'll absorb very much of it anyway. So along with finding our place in the rhythms of nature we'll learn fun things like spells and rituals. I can't promise the spells will make you the most popular person in class or that they'll make bullies cower at your every word (however tempting it is). But what I can promise is that you'll learn techniques and possibly gain a lifestyle that will change your attitude and outlook on life for the better.

First we'll learn a little about the history of Wicca and where the things we do come from. History wasn't my favorite subject either so I'll keep that short and try not to bore you too much. Like it or not, it's still a pretty essential jumping-off point in our studies. From there, we'll dive right into the core concepts that make up Wicca as a religion and practice. There's a lot of material to cover there and hundreds of books have been written on just about every topic we'll talk about. But everyone has to start somewhere, which means this won't be the last book on Wicca you pick up along the way.

Eventually we'll start talking about how and why magick works, and yes, we'll learn about spells too. Do yourself a favor though, and don't flip towards the back of the book for the spells. Getting some foundational work under your belt is essential before we start whipping our wands out. Just like in Driver's Ed, you don't pull out into the interstate before mastering the small roads in your neighborhood.

If I did my job right, you'll finish this book with a good understanding of what Wiccans do and specifically how to be Wiccan through the teenage years. With an open mind and an eagerness to learn, you'll be well on your way to learning the Craft of the Wise in no time.

Now, let's get started!

Chapter 1

Ancient Ways for Modern Days

Wicca as a complete religion is actually pretty new, but the roots of it come from old, and even ancient, sources. Tracing the history of every belief, ritual and practice is something way beyond the scope of this book. This is because Wicca today is a syncretic tradition, which pretty much means it's made of a bunch of different ideas that were restructured and mushed together to create something "new." But that doesn't make it any less valuable. All of the world's great religions come from ancient practices that existed before it. The artists of the new religions (yes, even Christianity is "new" in the scope of human history) all took things they liked from past traditions and added things of their own. It's a pretty genius idea because after all, all great artists copy each other's work. To look to Wicca's ancient roots, we have to go way back.

Stone Age Religion

To get our first glance at the ancient roots of Pagan religions, we can at least go back 30,000 years to the period known as the Upper Paleolithic. This is the time when scientists think religious rites like funerals and sacred burials began. Some of them even think the start of religious thought could have begun as far back as 300,000 years ago in the Middle Paleolithic, but we can't really be sure on much of the specifics. If you thought cave paintings were just primitive finger-paintings, think again! Much of the art discovered depicted different types of animals grazing alongside each other as the hunter closed in on its prey. Since such grand hunting opportunities were unlikely to be common, one could speculate that the art was used to honor the animal spirits, and maybe even to make the art a reality. Magick, anyone?

The Upper Paleolithic age was home to our oldest spiritual ancestors, the shamans. You might think of shamans as belonging to Native American peoples. However, the word shaman actually comes from North Asia and many of the ancient cultures had them, even if they didn't call them that. The shamans were essentially the first people to discover that the land held powers that could be tapped into by entering altered states of consciousness. They were valued in their communities for their ability to enter special relationships with the spirits that brought them the gifts of healing and prophecy. We'll go more into shamanism's relationship with Wicca and Paganism later on.

Another famous clue to ancient Paganism is the Venus sculptures, also a symbol of the Upper Paleolithic age. Figures like these featured images of females with overly emphasized breasts and large pregnant bellies. Although scientists can't agree on whether they were charms to ensure fertility or depictions of an ancient earth goddess, we can be certain the intentions were religious in nature.

Icons like the Venus continued to pop up throughout the Upper Paleolithic and into the Mesolithic period, where pottery for practical (not just religious) use became more common.

Things get really interesting as we move on and look at the Neolithic period, starting around 12200 BCE. This is the age when farming became prevalent and civilizations started springing up around the Fertile Crescent (the area between the Persian Gulf and Egypt). With civilization came the start of organized religion. Pantheons (organized systems of gods), temples, priests and priestesses, and systems of astrology and magick all began in this Bronze Age.

Our last look at what we'll call "the ancients" is in the Iron Age, around 1300 to 1200 BC. The myths and cultures of the gods and goddesses of the near east matured along with the cultures of the Celts, Greeks, Romans, and Scandinavians. This is the age where much of the lore on magick and sorcery comes from and the regions where the most interesting Pagan civilizations made history.

Ceremonialism and Secret Societies

From the ancient times we flash forward to the 16th and 17th centuries where a fraternal organization called Freemasonry grew up from mysterious and largely unknown origins. The Masons, though supposedly forbidden to discuss things like specific religious beliefs, take much of their structure and practices from the esoteric mystery schools of ancient times. If you walk into a Masonic temple today, the artistic influences of ancient Greece and Egypt are pretty obvious. Washington D.C., where I live, is home to one of the biggest Masonic temples in the United States and walking into it can make you feel like you're transported back to the age where temples to the gods and goddesses were commonplace. It's easy to see the draw for those of us who are attracted to those things.

The 16th century was also a popular time for astrology and certain forms of Christian mysticism, like the work done by Dr. John Dee, court astrologer to Queen Elizabeth I. Dee formed his own system of angelic magick along with his associate Edward Kelly. The complicated system they formed that we call Enochian is still in use today by those magicians daring enough to try and get the hang of it. In any case, Dee and Kelly are great examples of the type of magick practiced during this time in history that was deemed acceptable – under the guise of Christianity of course.

In the late 19th century we find three guys named William Robert Woodman, William Wynn Westcott, and Samuel Liddell MacGregor Mathers. All three of them were Freemasons and together they formed a new society called the Hermetic Order of the Golden Dawn (or just Golden Dawn for short). The founders of the Golden Dawn based their organizing structure off of Freemasonry but with a nice advantage – they allowed women to join!

The Golden Dawn had different levels of study where they learned things like Qabalah (a system of Hebrew mysticism), astrology, tarot, alchemy, and astral travel. Their courses of study were so detailed that they formed the backbone of so many magical traditions that arose after its creation, including Wicca.

However well-structured it was, the order splintered in disagreement on the arrival of a controversial new member by the name of Aleister Crowley in 1898. Crowley was controversial not only for his bisexuality (which on its own at the time was certainly a big no-no), but also for his recreational use of drugs and flashy showmanship. Even though the man was a bit of an eccentric, his tireless work in advancing magickal knowledge ended up being a huge help to the great esoteric thinkers of his time. One of those thinkers was a British civil-servant by the name of Gerald Gardner.

Gerald Gardner and the Birth of Wicca

Did you know that as recently as the 1940s, you could still be tossed in jail for practicing witchcraft? Even though the law wasn't used very much by then, the Witchcraft Act of 1735 was still alive and loomed over the witches of England as a ball and chain. It didn't make much sense either. Even though the practice of magick was still pretty hidden, the practice of spiritualism was all the rage in England and beyond. Spiritualists believe that the spirits of the dead have a lot to teach the living, and so they contact them through methods like mediumship and séances. Although many people were really serious about spiritualism, it was also thought by many to be a form of entertainment, a hobby for the privileged wealthy. Regardless, the last person to be prosecuted under the Act was a woman by the name of Helen Duncan, charged for her claims of summoning spirits. In this case, you could call this the last official "witch trial" under the Act.

The Witchcraft Act was pretty broad, so why weren't people like spiritualists and members of Freemasonry more frequently persecuted? The answer is up for debate and probably multi-layered, but I believe its part language and part money. People who weren't spiritualists didn't have any pre-made idea about what the practice was so they didn't really have much to compare it to. It wasn't a taboo buzzword like the word "witchcraft" was. And since high-society rich people were into it, it wasn't challenged all that often. Money talks.

With the Witchcraft Act still in place, interests like spiritualism and esoteric clubs like Freemasonry and the Theosophical Society continued to draw in interest across Europe and beyond. I guess you could say that people were hungry for assistance from the beyond and many weren't satisfied with the standard religion they were getting from the Church. And who could blame them? From 1935-1945, World War II was a very terrifying reality for the people of the time. And when the war ended in 1945, people had a renewed sense of hope for the approaching mid-point in the century. The magickal thinkers of the time must have sensed that they were on the verge of a great turning point in esoteric history.

A huge step in that turning point came in 1951 when the old Witchcraft Act was finally repealed and replaced with the Fraudulent Mediums Act. It's likely that the government of the time didn't see the need for such a silly and outdated law to exist in a country that was pushing the idea of liberty and freedom. And of course the repeal had some help from those organized esoteric societies.

I don't think the British government realized that repealing the old Witchcraft Act would actually encourage real witches to pop up and make themselves known. And how could they? Even people interested in such things had to jump through hoops and know exactly the right people to get any decent information on the topic. And until the Act was repealed, it was difficult to even find witchcraft-based fiction, much less any how-to manual! And after all, witches were just part of England's superstitious past, or so they thought.

One of the people who came in to challenge that idea was Gerald B. Gardner. Gardner was the founder of what we practice as Wicca today, although he didn't even call what he did "Wicca." The word Wicca actually came about later since Gardner simply called his practice witchcraft. In fact, when Wicca was first mentioned, it only had one C in its name anyway! There is much speculation on where the word Wicca comes from, but most believe it was coined by Gardner's early followers as simply a derivative for the term "witch." Back then, the two words were pretty much interchangeable.

Gardner retired from his work in civil service in 1936 and returned to his home country of England to join a secret society, just like the ones we talked about earlier. The society he joined was called the Rosicrucian Order Crotona Fellowship. It was through this group that he claimed to have met the infamous New Forest Coven. In 1939, he was initiated by them. Once again we find a sketchy history since no one has proved or disproved a complete history of Gardner's initiating coven, or if it even existed in the first place! Detractors to Gardner claim the New Forest Coven was an invention of his to give a historic foundation for the folkloric practices of witchcraft that Gardner was attempting to restructure and revive as a complete system. Whatever the case may be, he continued his work mostly unbothered and began forming the skeleton of what would eventually become the Wiccan religion.

In 1945, Gerald Gardner moved to London and published a fictional novel called *High Magic's Aid* in 1949. Remember, this was a couple of years before the Witchcraft Act was repealed so Gardner had to publish his first witchcraft book under the guise of fantasy. But to the trained reader, one could pick out the practices of the witch cult that Gardner and his covenmates practiced in real life. It's even thought that Gardner passed out copies of *High Magic's Aid* to prospective initiates to gauge their comfort levels. The book itself didn't sell very well, but I suspect this didn't really bother him very much.

1949 was also the year Gardner met Aleister Crowley. We don't know much about their meetings but they must have taken a liking to each other since Gardner became a frequent visitor of his and eventually joined his magickal society, the Ordo Templi Orientis. All of this happened late in Crowley's life and he was likely desperate to see the OTO succeed and thrive beyond the years of his own life. So as a result, Crowley issued a charter proclaiming that Gardner had the right to the ritual material of the OTO and to initiate members into the order on his own. This is important because much of the material that ended up going into the early drafts of the Gardnerian Book of Shadow's was re-tooled OTO rituals with the names of Pagan gods inserted throughout.

Jumping forward once again to the '50s and the repeal of the Witchcraft Act, Gardner was free to publish whatever he darn well liked. So in 1954, he published his first non-fiction book, *Witchcraft Today*. As you can imagine, Gardner's witchcraft revival was quite a shock to the people of England, and the media was all abuzz with reporting on Britain's most famous witch.

After *Witchcraft Today* was published, all bets were off. Gardner was known all throughout England and beyond as Britain's witchcraft man. People would use Gardner as a point of contact for their interest in the occult studies (occult just means hidden, by the way). This was all probably very exciting for him, knowing that his desire to revive the old ways of the witch was succeeding. However, Gardner didn't do it alone. We already know that Gardner had help from the OTO in creating Wicca's rituals, but there were a few other important characters who played a role in shaping them up to what we have today.

Doreen Valiente and the Book of Shadows

In the winter of 1952 a woman named Doreen Valiente appeared in Gardner's life. Having a sincere interest in magickal studies from a young age, she originally heard about the witchcraft revival going on in her area of England from a popular weekly magazine. And so it was that Valiente wrote to a contact listed in the article who passed her information along to Gardner. In winter of that year, the two met in the living room of Gardner's witchcraft partner, a woman named Dafo. Valiente describes her first meeting with Gardner in her book *The Rebirth of Witchcraft*:

> *"We seemed to take an immediate liking to each other. I realized this man was no time-wasting pretender to occult-knowledge. He was something different from the kind of people I had met in esoteric gatherings before. One felt that he had seen far horizons and encountered strange things; and yet there was a sense of humor about him and a youthfulness, in spite of his silver hair."*

The following summer, Valiente was initiated as a witch and eventually became Gardner's most trusted priestess. Valiente shared Gardner's vision of making witchcraft accessible to more people who had an interest in learning about it and her youthful intelligence was exactly what they needed to propel it forward.

In the early days of Wicca, every initiate had to hand copy the Book of Shadows word for word. As creepy as it might sound at first, a book of shadows is simply a magickal diary of sorts, used to contain the formula and results for the witch's spells. We'll talk more about them later on in this book since they're much different than they used to be when Valiente first wrote hers.

While Valiente was copying the book, she noticed that many of the rituals were arranged in ways that looked very much like Aleister Crowley's work. Remember, Crowley was quite the controversial man, even at the end of his lifetime. Valiente quickly realized that the only way to make the rituals more approachable was to cut out the Crowley-style wording and replace it with something more user-friendly. Luckily, Valiente was a brilliant poet! Using her gift with words, she added her own flare to the Gardnerian Book of Shadows which resulted in some of the most beautiful and poetic liturgy Wicca has seen since. It seems her feminine touch was exactly what the rituals of Wicca needed and I can only imagine how they would look if she didn't take on the project.

But all good things must come to an end and eventually Valiente become annoyed with Gardner's increasing media attention, worried it would compromise the safety and integrity of the group. She writes in *The Rebirth of Witchcraft:*

> *"As the coven's High Priestess, I felt that by speaking to the press, Gardner was compromising the security of the group and the sincerity of his own teachings."*

Apparently the disagreement was bad enough to cause the two to peacefully split and in 1957 she formed her own coven that she priestessed over for seven years.

Robert Cochrane and the 'Traditional Witches'

1964 was a big year for Doreen Valiente. It was the year both Gerald Gardner and Valiente's mother died. However, while attending a solstice event that same year, she came to befriend a charismatic man named Robert Cochrane. Cochrane, just like Gardner, was an interesting guy. He claimed to practice a type of witchcraft that was entirely different from Gardner's line. He claimed to practice a form of traditional witchcraft that lived on in an unbroken line for centuries before him.

Even though Cochrane had no evidence to support his claim of a hereditary line, witchcraft was still practiced earlier than the arrival of Gerald Gardner and Wicca. The type of witchcraft practiced by Robert Cochrane was less ceremonial than Gardner's

Wicca and preferred to place a focus on more of the shamanic practices of native England and other European cultures. He was considered a cunning-man, wise in the way of herbs and spirits of the forest. He was what we now typically call a "traditional witch," a term non-Wiccan witches use to describe their practices. Traditional witches don't usually see witchcraft as a religion, but rather a practice that can have an optional religious tradition attached to it depending on the practitioner.

Valiente was attracted to Cochrane's Craft and their disinterest in drawing media attention was a welcome relief to the over-burdened Valiente. She also admired the tradition's commitment to working in nature. She later commented that *"Cochrane believed in getting close to nature as few Gardnerian witches at the time seemed to do."* She was quickly initiated into his coven, the Clan of Tubal Cain, but later broke away from it. Valiente became disillusioned with Cochrane's constant bullying of the Gardnerians, along with a few other unsavory character traits. The funny thing is, many people believe that Cochrane took much of his work from Gardner who was thought to have initiated him years prior to the formation of his own coven!

In any case, Cochrane's work was influential on Valiente and so the more naturalistic practices of traditional witchcraft wove their way into many of the later lines of Gardnerian Wicca. A line of Wicca similar to Gardnerian, although more of a split from it, is Alexandrian Wicca. Alexandrian Wicca was started by British witch Alex Sanders and its practice is so similar to Gardnerian, most outsiders would notice only small differences like a few of the tools and some of the symbols. Alexandrian Wicca is also similar to Gardnerian in that it's an initiatory-only line, meaning you have to be initiated by an Alexandrian Wiccan to become one. From Alexandrian and Gardnerian Wicca, dozens of different sects emerged, beginning the big web of diverse forms of Wicca that we have today.

Coming to America

Although Wicca and witchcraft were quickly increasing in popularity throughout the British Isles, it took a little longer for it to reach America. Thank goodness for the arrival of Raymond Buckland in the '60s, or who knows how long it would have taken Wicca to reach the States.

Raymond Buckland was a native Englishman but immigrated to Brentwood, Long Island, in the United States with his family in 1962 when he was 28. He grew up around a family of spiritualists, so the occult world was something he was pretty familiar with at an early age. Although spiritualism was the bread and butter of his family, Buckland craved something more, a religion he could really sink his teeth into. Shortly after moving to America, he read Gardner's book *Witchcraft Today*. It seems he found exactly what he was looking for in discovering Wicca. After reading the book and learning more about the witchcraft revival happening in England, Buckland wrote and chatted on the phone with Gardner and the two men quickly became friends. Gardner eventually came to trust Buckland so much that he made him a sort of spokesperson for Wicca in the United States. Whenever someone from the States would contact Gardner, he would pass it along to Buckland for a response. It's a pretty clever system when you think about how much earlier in the century this was before the arrival of email.

Buckland flew to Scotland with his wife in 1963 where he was initiated by Monique Wilson, Gardner's High Priestess at the time. Gardner himself attended the rite.

Wicca (along with many different Pagan paths) really took off after Buckland started spreading it in 1964. He wasn't really interested in press attention like Gardner was though. Buckland grew his own personal coven very slowly, which was likely an attempt at maintaining the integrity of Wicca and the coveners who practiced it.

Wicca and all forms of Paganism coming into America in the

mid-'60s was a move so perfect it could almost be confused as an intentional strategy. The rise of the hippie movement and feminism mushed together with the Pagans of the time, a trend that continued well into the '70s. With so many people learning about the Pagan revival, different traditions began shooting out all over the United States and Gardnerian Wicca quickly went from being a dominant path within Wicca to one of its minorities. Different traditions of witchcraft (both Wiccan and not) drew in numbers from every side of the coast.

The Feri tradition begun by Victor and Cora Anderson in California was one of the earliest formal traditions of witchcraft practiced in the United States. Victor Anderson began teaching the tradition (at the time known as "Vicia" or just "the Craft") as early as the '40s and began formally initiating students into the tradition in the '50s. Although Feri isn't a part of Wicca, it's interesting to know that these small numbers of Feri practitioners were reviving witchcraft on the West Coast even earlier than the time Wicca was born over in England. And it's a good thing they did because Feri was influential on a number of people who later went on to become influential teachers themselves, like Starhawk.

Starhawk, based in the San Francisco area of California, is a leader of her own tradition of witchcraft call Reclaiming. She published a book called *The Spiral Dance* in 1979 which was groundbreaking for students of Paganism across America. The book outlines the foundation of Wicca, non-Wiccan traditions like Feri, and the rise of the emerging Goddess movement going on at the time.

Being a student of the Feri tradition myself, I could go on about that forever. But we've been talking about history for quite a large number of pages so let's speed it up! We'll close out our little history lesson with the decades following the explosion of Wicca and Paganism across the US in the '80s, '90s, and two-thousands.

By the '80s, the hippie movement had pretty much all but faded out, even though feminism was still going strong. Witchcraft on its own was still spreading like crazy as traditions and organizations formed in the '70s really began to dig their roots deep and mature. It's in this decade where we find organizations like the Church of All Worlds, Covenant of the Goddess, School of Wicca, and Circle Sanctuary expanding their numbers and taking on special projects like Pagan rights.

One special event in the '80s was the court case Dettmer v. Landon. In the case, a Wiccan prisoner named Herbert Daniel Dettmer sued the Virginia Department of Corrections for the right to access Wiccan ritual tools in the prison. The prison claimed Wicca wasn't a religion at all, but rather just a jumbled-up collection of random occult practices. Dettmer won in federal court but was appealed in the Fourth Circuit court. Unfortunately, the Fourth Circuit ruled against Dettmer this time and he lost. The good part is that when the Fourth Circuit ruled, they ruled with the statement that Wicca was indeed a proper religious tradition protected by the 1st Amendment. The case lost because they didn't think his right to practice was interrupted by the denial of the tools. Either way, we find the first instance where the federal government made an official claim about the validity of Wicca in America. This set a great precedent for Wiccans across the nation and opened the way for other cases on Pagan rights to come after.

Wicca experienced a huge turning point in the '80s with the growth of solitary practice. That is, Wicca that's okay to perform alone without a coven. Although there are a bunch of ways Wicca started becoming accessible outside of covens, solitary practitioners have one person in particular to thank: Scott Cunningham. Cunningham was a big proponent of making Wicca accessible to wider numbers of people who wanted to study it, but didn't have a coven (or didn't want one) to work with. In the early '80s he published several books putting forth

Wiccan spirituality and practice that's still known to this day to be very "user-friendly." His most important work came in 1988 when he published *Wicca: A Guide for the Solitary Practitioner*. As the ideas from the book spread, solitary Wicca became an increasingly accepted form of practice. And by the end of the '80s and into the early '90s, it became the dominant form of Wicca to practice.

The '90s brought us the internet and ushered in the information age. Whatever accessibility we got from the books published in the '80s was nothing compared to the info prospective Wiccans had access to in the '90s. The internet truly changed the face of how Wiccans and Pagans interacted with each other and how early seekers learned about it. Excitement around Wicca was huge in the mid-'90s too. The media was really into making television shows and movies about witches like *The Craft* and *Practical Magic*. Sure, for many people the interest in Wicca that came about by movies was probably a phase for them, but there were many people who still picked it up as a serious practice after taking the time to learn more about it.

I won't lie; being a pre-teen during that time was part of my attraction to Wicca too. And you know what? I'm totally okay with that. Chances are, you may have picked up this book after seeing a witchy movie thinking, "Hey, maybe I can do that." Of course, I trust that you're smart enough to realize that real witches can't actually do things like fly through the air (physically anyway) and move objects with our mind. But still, you may have been drawn to it through the media because of its edgy, rebellious feel. And I'm cool with that too! The truth is, some adult Wiccans can get judgmental of young people who are drawn to the Craft because of movies or TV. I think it's none of their business why you're drawn to it. The important thing is that you're here, learning about what Wicca really is and searching for answers on your own.

At the time of writing, we're a couple years past the two-thousands. Scholars are still trying to unpack exactly what the '00s meant for Paganism in America and abroad. I see these decades as being the full emersion of Wicca into the mainstream. Every year since the millennium it seems like it gets easier and easier to tell someone you're Pagan, or especially Wiccan. Wiccans are fortunate in that we've had the most exposure to society, more than any other Pagan path, so I think it's easier for people to get a sense of who we are. Depending on the area (and cities do this more than small towns), you can casually say, "I'm Wiccan," and the other person has a good chance of knowing what you mean. They may not have any idea about the exact practices and beliefs of the religion, but they might have a friend or family member who is.

Many scholars think there could be as many as 1.5 million people identifying with some type of Pagan path in America. Wicca is still the largest of all the religions in modern Paganism, so that makes for quite a lot of Wiccans! The numbers for other countries are sketchy at best so there's really no telling how many Wiccans, Pagans, and witches there are all over the world. In fact, some religious scholars think Paganism makes up some of the fastest-growing group of religions in the world!

The '00s were a time where discrimination against nature-based religions was becoming more and more of a no-no in the US and the UK, and this is still the case today. Wiccan soldiers won the right from the Veterans Administration to have the pentacle placed on their gravestones. Military bases all over the country are setting aside specific places for Wiccans to gather together and worship. Pagan seminaries and schools are getting accredited to offer people professional degrees in topics like Contemporary Paganism, Pagan Counseling, and more. Wiccans and other Pagans participate in all the major interfaith events like the American Academy of Religion and the Parliament of World Religions. Just the other day I got an email announcing that the current vice president is a witch. If that isn't progress, I don't know what is.

And now we arrive at the present day, with you here, learning about Wicca possibly for the first time in your life. It's an exciting time for a young person to become Wiccan today. You get the privilege of studying the Craft in a time of mass acceptance and tolerance of our religion. You get access to more information than has ever been available to anyone before. And most exciting to me is seeing young people like teens and young adults taking on leadership positions in the Pagan community. But more on that later.

Who knows what the future will hold for Wicca and the other Pagan religions. But based on everything that's happened so far, I can only think we have totally awesome things in store. You're part of that history, too. Everything you learn and every step you take on your path weaves a new exciting thread into the tapestry of culture.

Chapter 2

The Gods and You

A Wiccan Creation Myth

Long ago before time, form, or even thought existed, there was the void. The void was so filled with nothing that we don't even have a name for it. There was no space, or even the beginnings of space. No sound, temperature, light, or dark. When I say nothing, I mean 100% nothing. Zip, zero, zilch.

Eventually the void began to soften around its edges a bit. The softening gave it texture and depth. With depth came the ability to move and organize. With all this happening, the movement of the void formed energy and color. The void became dense with all these untouchable things and began to turn dark. It turned itself into the very beginnings of what we might think of as space.

So space (with no "thing" in it by the way) began to ebb and flow around itself, its energy forming a consciousness, a central heart. This was the very first center point. If the void were a huge sheet of black poster-board, the new center point would be a tiny white dot in the center. As the void continued to move and coil around itself, it drew in more energy. All the energy of anything that existed in the void was pulled together.

Just as it seemed as though the void was slowing down and was no longer drawing energy into itself, it began to grow warm and radiate light. This was the first light, the first stirrings of consciousness. The center point was actually looking out to the rest of the void and seeing itself. It was seeing its heart and realizing that is existed. It became self-aware. And from the moment of that awareness, it exploded all around itself and extended outwards in all corners of the void, filling the void with consciousness, darkness, and light. That consciousness was the Great Goddess.

As the Goddess moved, still cloaked in shadow, she began to take on form. Excited by her own movement, she began to dance. As she danced, her feet kicked up the dust of space and formed the stars. Through the stars, the Goddess knew beauty and realized that was just the thing she wanted her space to be filled with. So she created more and more, filling every corner of the void until it was most certainly no longer a void. It was the starry space.

As she danced, she began to feel a yearning for more. She wanted a companion to join in her dancing, someone to love and celebrate with. So with the light of the burning stars and the limitless love from her deep heart, she formed a new being, the God. The God, though born in his infancy, went through a metamorphoses and transformed himself into adulthood.

Together the Goddess and God danced. And as they danced they created more things, including the planets, gravity, and solar systems so the planets could dance around each other, just like they did. And even with all this creation going on, they yearned for more beauty, more light. So through their loving union, they brought forth the life-giving planets, like Earth.

The Goddess and God turned to Earth and made it their most beautiful creation. The Goddess cried tears of joy for their work together which fell down as rain and formed the oceans and rivers. Through her laughter, the land masses rumbled and began to take shape. And through the deep love of the Goddess and her consort, the hot molten core of the Earth was formed at its center. The God roared with laughter and from the sound of this, the first organisms were sparked with life deep in the ocean.

The Goddess and God continued to dance, love, sing and laugh as they created more creatures, animals to populate the Earth. Earth became not just a place of brilliant beauty, but a planet of life with its own creatures, having their own thoughts. The birth of those first creatures was coupled with the birth of the spirits of nature. The spirits of nature were present within every plant and animal, as well as separate entities in their own way. Together the spirits, the creatures, and the land formed complete ecosystems and developed patterns to repopulate themselves.

For a while, the Goddess and God were satisfied. But it didn't take long for them to feel that yearning once again. Something felt missing, like planet Earth still had the potential to hold more. So gathering up the energy from their love, the energy of the planet, and the creatures, they formed the first humans. The Goddess taught the humans how to love and the God taught the humans how to survive in their earthly forms. Together they gently guided the first humans on how to live peacefully upon the Earth.

As humanity grew, the Goddess and God began to see a need for special people on the Earth to help the humans remember their lessons. They needed people who would remember the Old Ways of nature and the lessons of the spirits. So reaching from the depths of their hearts and pouring love into some of the humans, along with the gifts of the spirits of nature, the first magick-workers were born. These were the first shamans and witches, sent to the Earth to be healers and teachers.

Though all seemed lovely in this world for a time, the free will the Goddess and God gifted to the humans wasn't always used in ways that were kind and helpful. So civilizations sprang up and some parts of humanity began to forget their origins. They began to view the Earth as the soulless resource for food and energy and nothing more. The Old Ways were being forgotten.

But still, living on the edges of the villages and in the temples of the God, the magick-workers continued to honor the Old Ways and keep the balance of the Earth. They celebrated the turning of the seasons and the cycles of the lives of the gods. They helped humanity remember where they came from. And even though they haven't always been appreciated (even to the point of terrible abuse), they continue to exist in many forms in many cultures. In every generation they continue to be born, waking up and realizing their purpose on this planet. So take heart, for you are the latest in that long line of generations. We are the stuff of stars.

The Wiccan Mythos

You might have noticed that at the start of that story, I called it "a" Wiccan creation myth rather than "the" Wiccan creation myth. The way every Wiccan tradition tells the creation myth is a little different, although each one contains a few core similarities. In most myths, the Goddess is seen as coming into existence first. She's literally responsible for birthing everything that came after her. That's why you'll often hear her called different titles like "Great Mother" or "Mother Goddess." All Wiccans honor the Goddess, even if they give her different names and view her in different forms.

In the myth, we have this image of the "void" as being the starting point, the point in time where the universe got its Goddess. Many traditions call this "Spirit" and some even honor it along the same level as the Goddess. Spirit and the Goddess are seen as interconnected parts of each other, neither being possible without the other.

Next, we see the birth of the God. This is where things can get tricky depending on who you learn from. Most traditions believe that the God was literally born from the "womb" of the Goddess. But if the womb of the Goddess is space itself, how is that even possible? Well, that's where the poetry of the myth comes into play. The myth of course is not seen as totally literal (like how some Christians read the Bible). Instead, we recognize that myths are stories that help us understand things that would totally fry our puny human brains if we could really see what was going on. The "realness" of the myths isn't as important as what they teach us about life and ourselves. The birth of a male god from a female goddess is an example of a poetic myth shared in many cultures all over the world, mimicking the birth of every baby human.

Finally, we see the creation of Earth, humanity, and the magickal people. In the myth I call them special and didn't mention the earliest civilizations of people who practiced Pagan religions. This is because even though all Wiccans and witches are Pagan (in the sense that they're polytheistic or have nature-based beliefs), not all Pagans are witches or Wiccan. Confusing? Think of it this way: all Catholics are performing a type of Christianity, which has many different sects within it. But not all Christians are Catholic. In the same way, all Wiccans are performing a type of Paganism. Paganism is a really broad term that could be applied to Wiccans, witches, Druids, heathens, and followers of native polytheistic practices. In the myth, witches are seen as a little separate from the rest of humanity. Although now witches are completely integrated into every function of society, that hasn't always been the case. Witches in all their cultures were usually seen as a little strange, living on the outside of the village and only approached for specific needs. When I say witches are special amongst the rest of humanity, I don't mean that we're better than anybody. In fact, many witches (and Wiccans for that matter) see their Craft as a way to assist and honor the whole of humanity. Personally, I believe that myself too.

Wiccan myths like the creation myth can be seen as taken from a bunch of different cultures from all over the world. The idea of the Goddess of the stars and space is definitely not something Gerald Gardner made up. Star goddesses were really popular all throughout the ancient Middle East. Ishtar, Astarte, Inanna, and Isis are all goddesses that have their original home in the stars, but take special attention to the Earth and what goes on here. After all, the Earth is made of star stuff too.

Dualism, Monism, and other Fun Words

Dualism: At its base, Wicca would be classified as a dualistic religion. Dualism means we can break down everything in our spiritual worldview as coming from the Goddess and God. We can see that in the creation myth, everything being born out of their love and union. Energy is often seen as dualistic in Wicca too. Dark and light, positive and negative are all dualistic ideas that Wiccans work with and explore. It's important to know that even though Wiccans view many things in the universe as two-sided, that doesn't mean we think one thing is "good" while another thing is "evil." Instead, energy is seen as neutral and can be made positive or negative depending on what the person does with it. The spider isn't evil because it eats the fly (although the fly might disagree). It's just doing what spiders do.

In a way, Christianity could be seen as dualistic too but in a very different way. Christians believe in an ultimate good (God) and an ultimate evil (the Devil). They both play huge and specific roles in the Christian mythology, usually warring against each other. Wiccans on the other hand don't believe in the concept of an absolute evil. There is no Devil in Wicca whatsoever. So it's kind of funny whenever a Christian accuses a Pagan of worshipping the Devil. It's like accusing an atheist of worshipping God. You cannot worship a god you don't believe exists.

Monism: If dualism represents things in the universe that are two-sided, then monism is the belief of something in the universe as one-sided. This is not to be confused with monotheism which is the belief in only one god. Wicca is unique because it's monist as well as dualist. Although the Goddess and God are totally unique in their own ways, they both came from a central point, spirit. Similarly, all the different goddesses of the world are seen as faces and aspects of a single main Goddess. Still with me here? Great! Let's move on...

Polytheism: This is an easy one. Polytheism is the belief in more than one god. Wicca is polytheistic because we honor both the Goddess and God as equally important. Also, many Wiccans honor other specific gods, the gods of ancient cultures. Like we've already discussed, most Wiccans who honor individual gods see them as aspects of the main one. So goddesses like Isis, Athena, Kali, and Aphrodite are all seen as "faces" or personalities of our main Goddess. The same is true with all the different gods, being aspects to the main God. Wicca's polytheism is pretty unique and many of the ancient cultures would consider our view of their unique gods as terribly inaccurate. To the ancient people, each god was seen as being a totally unique individual and not an aspect of anything else.

Today, there are still Pagan paths out there that have this belief. We would just simply call them "polytheists" or even "hard polytheists" to distinguish them from the "soft polytheism" of Wicca. There are hard polytheists for nearly every pantheon of gods. Greek polytheists are called Hellenics, Northern European polytheists are called Heathens, and so on.

Pantheism: This is the belief that there is spirit, or divine life, in every single thing on the planet. It means that the gods are all-encompassing and flowing through all things. Similar to pantheism is animism; the belief that all things in nature (living or not) have a spiritual essence inside them that is absolutely no different to their physical forms.

Language is difficult for us humans so don't try to unpack all those words and what they mean to Wicca all at once. In fact, Wiccan scholars are constantly debating what they mean to our religion and how much or little they apply. Words like these help us talk about our experiences and give a frame of reference, but they're still just words. In Wicca, your experience (whether you have words to describe it or not) is always the most important thing.

The Charge of the Goddess

Listen to the words of the Great Mother, who was of old also called Artemis; Astarte; Diana; Melusine; Aphrodite; Cerridwen; Dana; Arianrhod; Isis; Bride; and by many other names.

Whenever ye have need of anything, once in a month, and better it be when the moon be full, then ye shall assemble in some secret place and adore the spirit of me, who am Queen of all Witcheries.

There shall ye assemble, ye who are fain to learn all sorcery, yet have not won its deepest secrets: to these will I teach things that are yet unknown.

And ye shall be free from slavery; and as a sign that ye are really free, ye shall be naked in your rites; and ye shall dance, sing, feast, make music and love, all in my praise.

For mine is the ecstasy of the spirit and mine also is joy on earth; for my Law is Love unto all Beings.

Keep pure your highest ideal; strive ever toward it; let naught stop you or turn you aside.

For mine is the secret door which opens upon the Land of Youth; and mine is the Cup of the Wine of Life, and the Cauldron of Cerridwen, which is the Holy Grail of Immortality.

I am the Gracious Goddess, who gives the gift of joy unto the heart. Upon Earth, I give the knowledge of the spirit eternal; and beyond death, I give peace, and freedom, and reunion with those who have gone before. Nor do I demand sacrifice, for behold I am the Mother of All Living, and my love is poured out upon the earth.

Hear ye the words of the Star Goddess, she in the dust of whose feet are the hosts of heaven; whose body encircleth the universe; I, who am the beauty of the green Earth, and the white moon among the stars, and the mystery of the waters, and the heart's desire, call unto thy soul. Arise and come unto me.

For I am the Soul of Nature, who giveth life to the universe; from me all things proceed, and unto me must all things return; and before my face, beloved of gods and mortals, thine inmost divine self shall be unfolded in the rapture of infinite joy.

Let my worship be within the heart that rejoiceth, for behold: all acts of love and pleasure are my rituals. And therefore let there be beauty and strength, power and compassion, honor and humility, mirth and reverence within you.

And thou who thinkest to seek for me, know thy seeking and yearning shall avail thee not, unless thou know this mystery: that if that which thou seekest thou findest not within thee, thou wilt never find it without thee.

For behold, I have been with thee from the beginning; and I am that which is attained at the end of desire.

Using the Charge

The Charge of the Goddess is an early piece of Wiccan liturgy with several different variations. It's believed that Doreen Valiente, being a gifted poet, put together much of Charge that's used today.

Wiccans use the Charge as a reminder of the values we hold dear. It's a lovely poem that can teach us a lot about how Wiccans view the Goddess. Some parts might sound a little confusing or strange since it sort of reads like a puzzle in some ways. Here's a little cheat sheet you can use to start unlocking its meaning.

- Listen to the words... – The first stanza is a reminder that the Goddess has been known all throughout time by a million names and more.
- Whenever ye have need of anything... – The second stanza provides us with permission to let the Goddess know about our needs and desires. It says that as our leader and guardian, honoring her will help us.
- There shall ye assemble... – The Goddess can teach us magick and assist us in working with the powers.
- And ye shall be free from slavery... – This is a poetic reference to the witch persecutions of the past, but can also be thought of as a metaphor. Think of "slavery" as all those

things a stressful society throws at us like guilt, injustice, and hatred. The part about being naked at her rites is both literal and a metaphor. Early Gardnerian witches worked in the nude (skyclad), and some still do. These days most Wiccans work clothed so we can take "naked" to mean that we allow ourselves to be totally exposed to the Goddess. We bring our honesty and true faces to her. We give her our trust.

- For mine is the ecstasy... – A reminder that the Goddess is present in all things. And that because of this, we should seek out joy and practice kindness to everything on the Earth. Everything is connected.

- Keep pure your highest ideal... – Your will in life is very important. Set high goals and do what you need to do to get there.

- For mine is the secret door... – The Goddess brings life as well as death and she's there for us in both. "Immortality" here means that the soul never dies. The cauldron of Cerridwen represents the transformation of the soul, as reference to reincarnation.

- I am the Gracious Goddess... – This is a statement of all the things the Goddess brings us in life and death. It says that because she brings life to all things, there's nothing we could give her that she doesn't already have. Because of this, she doesn't demand sacrifice and pain like the God of Christianity.

- Here ye the words of the Star Goddess... – This is my favorite line. No really, it is. I have it tattooed on my arm! It's my favorite part of the Charge because it's a reminder of just how vast the Goddess's influence is. If stars are just the dust of her feet, she really is limitless. But she is also the Earth and the moon, which means she can be "small" for us, so we might know her more deeply than if she only lived in the stars.

- For I am the soul of nature... – Another reminder that all things that live and die are connected because they all come from the Goddess and go back to her. She's telling us to have no fear in life or death, because there's joy in all these things.
- Let my worship be within the heart... – The most important act of worship in Wicca is the worship you do with your heart. It's your right as a child of the Goddess to be happy.
- And you who thinkest to seek for me... – The Goddess is reminding us how important it is that we know ourselves before we can understand our relationship with anything else outside of us. We have to look for our own power within ourselves before we can go looking for it anywhere else.
- For behold... – The closing is another reminder that the Goddess is both our origin and destination. In a literal sense, we all come from the Earth and it's to the Earth we go once we've had our life.

Exercise – Journaling the Charge

Keeping a journal is a really important part of any daily practice in Wicca. Use the Charge of the Goddess as a journal prompt to help you understand its meaning on a deeper level. Try writing down one stanza a day and what it means to you. You could also draw or paint some pictures if you're better with visuals than words. Get creative! Art is a great way to unlock your inner goddess or god.

The Triple Goddess

Even after all this talk of the Goddess being one, two, and many, there are still more (equally important) ways Wiccans work with her. In particular, the Triple Goddess plays many roles in the Wiccan mythos and shows up frequently in our work. There are many goddesses in the ancient world that seem to have triple forms; Brigit, Hecate, and the Morrigan are all great examples if you're interested in going on to look at their lore.

In Wicca, the Goddess herself is seen as "triple" because of the three main stages she goes through in accordance with the moon cycle. The Goddess is associated with the moon just as the God is associated with the cycles of the sun. They each present themselves differently to us depending on the time of the month and the season in the year. The three phases of the Triple Goddess are:

Maiden – The young aspect of the Goddess in her carefree wild stage. The maiden is the stage of the moon when it's growing (waxing) from new to full. The maiden is all things bright and new, in addition to energetic and sometimes fierce. Many Wiccans imagine the maiden being like Artemis, the goddess of the hunt. Her bow is seen as the tiny sliver of the crescent moon as it grows.

Mother – The mother aspect embodies all things nurturing. She's gentle but firm, guiding us along our way just like any good mother would. The mother is the stage of the moon when it's completely full. We might look to goddesses like Gaia, Hera, and Isis to tell us more about what the mother is like.

Crone – The crone is a sometimes misunderstood phase of Goddess as she's in the days of her old age. The elderly aren't usually acknowledged for their wisdom and strength in our society today. Wiccans know that the crone (in both her goddess form and in elderly humans) is really important and that she has much to teach us, if we only listen. Goddesses like Baba Yaga or Grandmother Spider are good examples of the crone.

As we move through life, each of us (whether female or male) can connect with the Triple Goddess and learn the lessons she has to teach us. When I was very young, I connected best with the Goddess in her mother form. I needed that nurturing guidance at the time, someone to be a gentle force to help me through my early years. Right now in my mid-twenties, I tend to connect with the crone more. As I grow into full adulthood, she gives me the firm wisdom I need to make smart choices and set up a good future for myself. You might think it would make more sense for me to connect with the maiden when I was much younger and then move into working with the mother right now. The Goddess doesn't really work in planned patterns all the time. We have all these categories we put her in to help us better understand, but she still reveals her mysteries to us in the ways she sees fit.

Exercise – Triple Goddess Devotional

To honor the Triple Goddess, I like to do devotionals. Devotionals are exactly what they sound like – practices that show our devotion so we can develop a strong relationship with the gods.

Gather three candles and set them before you in a row. If you can't have candles, that's okay, just use stones. A light-colored stone for the maiden, a mix-colored (or gray) stone for the mother, and a dark stone for the crone. Light a candle (or hold the appropriate stone by your heart) for each phase of the Goddess at her time. Think about what the Goddess means to you in whichever aspect you're honoring.

Here are some words you can say while you do that:

For the maiden:

Lovely maiden who dances anew
open up the way
In joy and reverence I call to you
and bless you on this day.

For the mother:

Gracious mother of the moon
I greet you with my heart

Grant to me a special boon
as this new day I start

For the crone:

Grandmother Queen who rides night
send your wisdom here
I bless you now in the waning light
and draw your guidance near

Devotionals are easy and creative ways to talk to the Goddess and God consistently every day. Feel free to make your own, especially if you don't like my rhymes. I'm no poet but maybe you are. The gods like it when we use our inspiration to speak with them.

The Correspondences and Symbols of the Goddess

Correspondences are ways of matching up one thing with another. Wiccans use correspondences in just about every aspect of our rituals, especially magick. Since green is the color of leaves, we see green as a correspondence for the element of Earth. The Goddess and God have their own correspondences and symbols that we can use both in ritual and in daily life to connect with them. Here are a few of the Goddess's:

Spiral – The spiral is an ancient symbol of rebirth. It represents the journey the Goddess takes as she travels deep below the Earth during the changing seasons. When she descends below, we have fall and the spiral moves counter-clockwise. When she returns and arises, we have spring and the spiral moves clockwise.

Labyrinth – We might think of labyrinths as a type of spiral, but one that goes clockwise and counter-clockwise at the same time. Labyrinths can be found all over the world etched in the ground and people walk the lines of them for peace and to contemplate their problems. Last year, I discovered that my local park has a labyrinth made of stone in the center of the park. I go there once a month to walk its pattern and think about the weeks ahead.

Triple Moon – Many Wiccans consider the triple moon "the" definitive symbol of the Goddess. The triple moon consists of a left-facing crescent moon on the left, a full moon in the center, and a right-facing (like a "C") crescent moon on the right. All three of these are put together in a row to make the triple moon)0(. It represents the three aspects of the maiden, mother, and crone.

Egg – Eggs are a symbol of fertility and are sacred to the Goddess in her mother aspect. Have you ever wondered why people dye eggs at Easter? This is actually an ancient Pagan practice that honors the fertile Goddess during the spring equinox.

Cup/Cauldron – We'll learn more about the cup and cauldron as tools later in the book, but they're certainly powerful symbols of the Goddess. They represent her cosmic womb where we all came from. There are many myths and legends associating the cauldron with goddesses and figures of transformation and rebirth.

Colors – Different traditions have different ways of corresponding colors to the Goddess and God. The colors system I like to use associates the Goddess with silver (the moon), black (night), red (her life-blood), and blue (the primordial ocean). I also associate the rainbow with the Goddess, since it's a trick of the light caused by her life-giving rains.

There are certainly many many more symbols you could give the Goddess, especially when you look at the many goddesses of ancient cultures. Take a look at the everyday symbols around you. What symbols would you give the Goddess that you'd include here? Try recording them in your journal and see which symbols make themselves known to you.

The God

As we read in the creation myth, the Goddess isn't the only part of the divine in Wicca. The God is companion, lover, and friend to the Goddess and their journey together shifts the tides of the seasons on Earth. All of the ancient goddess-revering cultures had gods in the mix too. Some of the earliest depictions of the God could be thought of as those early cave-wall drawings of the mighty beasts of the hunt.

The God sometimes had a tough time getting equal footing with the Goddess in Wicca. Many people who come to Pagan faiths come from super-repressive Christian churches. It's in these churches that people are often taught that God is solely male and that God is a man you should be absolutely terrified of...for your own good of course. "The fear of God" is a phrase many people who come from these backgrounds are familiar with. If you ask converts from Christianity to Wicca why they left the Church, you'll probably hear that they were tired of having a relationship with God based on fear. The ancient people had a solemn and respectful reverence for the gods, but they never felt enslaved or subjugated by them like some monotheistic religions feel today.

Fear is the main reason we get images like the Devil today. In the Church, we're taught that fearing God is in our best interest because it's better to fear him and win salvation, than to not fear him and face the Devil. It's actually a pretty strange idea when you look at the other religions of the world. This concept of a "good" God who will toss you into a place of torment with another god that's evil is relatively new and was quite foreign to people when the idea was proposed.

Because of the newness of this totally good/totally evil religion, early Christians had to find creative ways to convince people that the male gods they worshipped were actually the

Devil in disguise! Pan, a famous Greek god of nature, is a great example of this. Pan has many traits often associated with what we think of today as a Devil. He's a goat god so his feet are hooves, his head has horns, and he has a tail. And Pan wasn't the only one. There are many gods in different cultures throughout the Mediterranean and the British Isles that have characteristics like these.

When Wiccans call upon and honor the God, we're recognizing that original primal God of the forest before all the fear came into play. Wiccans don't need to fear our God because we can have a direct relationship with him, just like the Goddess. Through learning the many faces of the God, we learn more about how to reclaim the old God once more. Let's go over some of those faces:

The Horned One – When people unfamiliar with Wicca hear the name "horned one", they sometimes get a little nervous (there's that old Christian fear coming into play). But think about who the horned gods actually were to the ancient people and you'll get a good feel of who they are today. We've already mentioned Pan, the wild and youthful god of nature and the woods. Another horned god who was so special he was called upon by early Gardnerian Wiccans is Cernunos. Cernunos is a Celtic deity with mysterious origins. Although scholars don't know much about his origins, his art shows him with mighty horns, surrounded by the animals of the woods. The horned one is the aspect of the God we call upon for all things relating to the powers of the Earth.

Sun King – We'll learn more about the sun king face of the God when we talk about the sabbats, but it's still important to mention him here. As the Goddess corresponds to the moon, so does the God correspond to the sun. Sun king gods are also honored for their gifts of illumination, clarity, and inspiration, such as the god Apollo.

Harvest God – Again, the harvest gods will be discussed in

length when we talk about sabbats. The harvest gods were extremely important to many ancient people, and still are today. The god of the harvest ensures that we have enough food to eat for the coming year. It's certainly a huge responsibility!

Trickster/Magician – The trickster and magician serve similar functions so I like to group them together. These aspects of the God can be misunderstood and often ignored. But trickster gods like Loki from the Norse or Coyote from the Native Americans teach us important lessons about life. They challenge us to see beyond what's right in front of us. Those who dare to make the extra effort are rewarded with great wisdom or power.

Lord of Death – The God as death might be seen as the most obvious equivalent to the crone aspect of the Goddess. Gods of death are responsible for keeping a balance between the world of the living and the spirits. The death aspect is comforting, giving relief to those in pain at the end of their lives and protection for the souls as they transition into new states of being. Hades from the Greek and Osiris from the Egyptians are popular examples of gods of death.

Hero – Although sometimes seen in god-form and sometimes in human-form, the hero is an important aspect of the God all throughout ancient religion and literature. He is Herkules, completing difficult missions to fulfill his destiny. He is also Arthur, questing for the Holy Grail and meeting the challenges brought to his kingdom.

There are many more aspects to the God that could certainly fill up their own books (and many such books exist). It's also important to know that although these are all images commonly associated with the God, there are certainly goddesses from all over the world that fill these roles as well.

Exercise – Masks of the God
All of the above aspects of the God are also called "masks".

They're different faces of our God that tell different stories. We develop our relationship with the God based on how we interact with these masks as well as the masks we use ourselves.

Make your own mask representing one of these aspects. Use any material you like, although paper and some colored pencils will do just fine. This is no kid's activity, I can assure you. The practice of mask-making to connect with the gods is a powerful and ancient one. Wiccan covens will sometimes do this as a practice on Samhain, burning the masks in the sabbat bonfire at the end of the ritual. You can either burn your mask once you're done with it, or keep it to use again. Try it on and notice how it makes you feel. Does putting on the trickster mask make you feel playful and fun? Would a harvest mask make you feel generous? Record your experiences in your journal.

The Correspondences and Symbols of the God

The God has just as many symbols associated with him as the Goddess does. Here are a few of his:

Antlers – Representative of the horned god in all his aspects. Especially revered by the ancient Celts, antlers represent the God in all his wild forms.

Arrow - Symbolizes the god of the hunt and the ancient need for survival and defense. Many cultures believe that the gods taught humanity how to make and use weapons to defend their civilizations.

Circle and Crescent – Similar to the Triple Goddess symbol. When you say the phrase "the God symbol" in Wicca, it probably means this symbol. A simple circle with a crescent moon (points up) resting on top of it. The circle is the sun and the crescent in this case can either represent the God supporting the Goddess, or the antlers on top of the head of the God.

Crown – The crown represents the ancient sacred kings. Chosen kings who were picked to represent the gods on Earth, ensuring the fertility of the land. The crown is a symbol of sovereignty and represents the Wiccan's ability to be in control of their own life without being at the mercy of anyone else. Many goddesses are also seen with the crown.

Trident – The trident is a triple-forced spear. If you've ever seen an image of Poseidon or Neptune, you're probably familiar with the trident. It's also carried by Shiva, the great god of Hinduism. The trident often serves similar functions as the scepter or staff.

Maypole – The prime symbol of the Wiccan sabbat Beltane, the maypole has fertility associations and is pretty common to people of the British Isles as well as the Americas. We'll learn more about the maypole later when we talk about Beltane.

Colors – Since the God rules over everything relating to the light and the sun, it's no surprise that his colors would be yellow, orange, and gold primarily. Green is another God color, because of his guardianship of all things in nature. Along the same thread, purple is a God color because of his associations with grapes and the wine (the Greek god Dionysus is responsible for that one).

The Gods of Youth

What I love about Wicca (and all Pagan religions for the matter) is that the gods are relatable to us on a human level. We can describe them with characteristics and features that help us identify who they are and who we are in relation to them.

The great thing about the gods is that they're ever-changing. There isn't just some old man god sitting up in a cloud somewhere who doesn't understand our unique individual struggles. Instead, there are as many aspects to the Pagan gods as there are people on the planet. And yes, there are gods that specifically identify with teens! It might sound crazy, but there are many many young gods out there who have fabulous stories of overcoming the obstacles presented to them because of their age. I love learning about the gods of youth because they can inspire us to be great in everything we do.

Learning their stories and who they are is a great way to help you identify with the gods within. Here are a few of my favorite gods of youth that you might be interested in too:

- Persephone is the beloved Greek goddess of nature and the Underworld. Her mother Demeter is responsible for the changing of the seasons and the fertility of the land. Many people consider Persephone a type of rebel goddess. While in her youth, she ran off with the mysterious god of the Underworld, Hades. While there, she ate seeds from the pomegranate fruit that bound her to that land for half of the entire year. In the grief of missing her daughter, Demeter casts the Earth into the cold seasons until Persephone rises up and returns. She represents youthful curiosity and the bond between a mother and her child, even if they don't always get along or understand each other.
- Aradia is the half-human, half-god daughter of the goddess Diana. Aradia's story was popularized by a man named Charles Leland who wrote a book called *Aradia: The Gospel of Witches*. In his book, Leland describes how Aradia was sent to Earth to teach magick to humanity and free the magick-workers from their captors. She's another rebel-goddess and represents the spirit of independent thought and the search for freedom and justice.
- Nimue is one of my favorite youthful goddesses, although not many people are familiar with her. She's one of the gods of the Anderson Feri tradition of Witchcraft and represents all things that are wild and innocent. Her symbol is the green snake, representing regeneration and new life.
- Dian Y Glas or the "Blue God" is another deity from the Anderson Feri tradition and can be thought of as the twin

to Nimue. The Blue God represented all things youthful and vital. He's often depicted as the Peacock Angel Melek Taus of the Yazidi belief system.

- Antinous is now considered a god but got his start as the young lover of the Roman emperor Hadrian. After Antinous's death, people who loved his story began to revere him as a god. As a result, a huge cult centered on his worship sprung up around the Roman Empire. Part of his worship included Olympic-like games of swimming and racing. Gaming in honor of Antinous was unique because the contests usually involved competitions of music and literature. Antinous can be thought of as a god of youth and culture, helping us to find our unique calling.
- Taliesin began his life as a young servant named Gwion Bach. Gwion was servant to the Welsh goddess Cerridwen. That all changed when three drops of a powerful potion from Cerridwen's cauldron gave him instant wisdom and the powers of transformation. In his transformation he became Taliesin, the gifted bard. Taliesin represents the daring courage that it takes young people to succeed in the world today.

These are just a few small examples of the many gods of youth from a few of my favorite traditions. If you explore the gods on your own, you'll undoubtedly find one that matches up with where you are in your life right now.

Getting to Know the Gods

Many teens who come to Wicca come to it from a different religion. Maybe you grew up Christian and weren't satisfied with the Church, or you just wanted to develop a spiritual practice that gave you more than what you had before. One of my favorite things about Wicca is that it encourages you to develop your own personal relationship with the divine. There's no middle man or anything else standing in your way of talking to God (or Goddess). Sure we have priests and clergy, but their job isn't to put you in touch with the gods – that's up to you!

Even though I started practicing Wicca at a really young age, it still felt strange working with these gods that felt so new to me. Part of it was guilt from the churches I had been to. They pounded into me this idea that only they could get me access to the divine and without them, I could never have any real relationship with God. That all changed when I really started getting to know the Wiccan gods.

I'll never forget my first solitary ritual to commune with the Goddess. It was a full moon, but still early enough in the day for there to be light. I gathered up some basic supplies for a ritual and headed out to the woods behind my house. It was a chilly winter day and the woods were quiet, except for the chirping of birds and the tree branches breaking under my feet.

I found a small clearing in the woods and laid all my supplies out. I wanted to do everything "by the book" and was really nervous about screwing something up. I carefully counted out my supplies: a candle, a match, my representation of the Goddess (a printed image of the Egyptian goddess Isis), and some incense. One by one, I set up my space as my little beginner book instructed. I took a break and began connecting with the nature surrounding me as I prepared to begin the first steps of my simple ritual.

Before I could speak, I felt this wonderful presence overcome me. It was this really nice feeling of safety and assurance. The trees swayed around me, the birds stopped chirping, and the delicious smells of the woods came alive. All the nervousness of what I was about to do fell away. It's hard to explain and it's not like anything "supernatural" happened. To the opposite effect, everything was perfectly natural. I felt like I was exactly where I was meant to be at that time. My surroundings seemed to be responding to my every breath as I took in the wonderful feeling filling me.

Later after I finished my ritual I went back to my Craft teacher to ask her what that feeling was. I was confused because I felt all these magickal things before I had even started my ritual! She described it as the call of the Goddess. Many people get the call of the gods at different points in their life. Usually it marks a turning point, or happens in some situation where your intent to speak to the divine is triggered with an immediate response from them, even before you call out with your request. The gods can anticipate anything we do before we do it, so this feeling I got before my ritual was the gods telling me, "Relax, everything will be okay."

This is really the heart of what the Goddess and God mean to Wicca. They aren't some scary council of stuck-up deities demanding our attention or forcing us to get everything right. They are a mother, a father, companions, teachers, guides, and friends. We get to know the gods just like we would get to know any other companions or friends. We talk, listen, and learn together. It's a mutual relationship that depends on both our participation and theirs.

In a way, everything we do in Wicca brings us closer to the gods. Our rituals, prayers, and magick never separate from them, even if we don't intentionally involve them in all of those things directly. Since they are a part of everything, there's no way we can't *not* be involving them in everything we do. That's the great part about Wicca being an animistic and pantheistic (remember those words?) religion. Since nothing in nature is separate from the divine, everything we do to connect with nature connects us with the Goddess and God.

Even though everything in our Craft is designed to bring us closer to the gods, there are specific things Wiccans do to make that connection stronger. Here are some of the easiest things you can do to start developing your relationship with the Goddess and God today:

- Talk to them – Chat to the gods every day. Whether it's in a special time and place, on the bus to school, or walking around the mall. The gods are always willing to listen to what we have to say. Talking out loud can help you keep track of the conversation, but it's not required. I talk to them while I'm sitting at my desk, going out for a morning jog, and even when I take my morning shower. They don't have to be detailed conversations. Just saying hello is good enough.

- Celebrate the holy days – The sabbats and full-moon celebrations of Wicca are the perfect time to set aside special personal celebrations of the gods. When you honor the gods on these special days, you're participating in a form of worship that's existed for thousands of years. That connection, to the history of the Pagan people before you, can help make your relationship stronger and more meaningful.

- Learn – Research the different gods and goddesses of ancient cultures all over the world. The simple act of learning about how people from all over viewed them is a great way to grow your connection to them. Start with an ancient culture that really interests you. For me, it was the ancient Greeks. When I couldn't read books about Wicca in my pre-teen years, I'd have my mother drop me off at my local library. Libraries have tons of books on mythology and ancient civilizations. You can also rent some really great mythology documentaries from the library on DVD or look up free videos online.

- Give thanks – Showing gratitude to anyone is a great way to develop trust and love. Think about the last time someone deeply thanked you for doing something nice for them. It probably gave you a great feeling and inspired you to do more. The gods react in the same way. Showing we're thankful opens us up to receive more blessings and strength along our path. Showing gratitude regularly is just practical. It helps you to notice those little unseen blessings that pop up all the time that we might not otherwise pay attention to.

We'll talk a lot about the gods throughout the rest of this book so you'll pick up a lot more information than what's presented here. The main thing to remember is that it's not enough to just learn about the gods, you have to experience them too. In the next chapter, we'll talk about exactly what Wiccans do and how those practices bring us power, strength, and connection with the gods. So enough talk about theory, let's get to the really fun stuff!

Chapter 3

Wiccan Practice

This chapter will look at the main core beliefs and practices of Wiccans today. They're what really define Wicca as a spiritual practice and ground it into the material world. Wiccans do all sorts of interesting things to attune with the seasons, celebrate nature, and perform magick. Some of them you might already be familiar with from one source or another, and others might be totally new to you.

This is the "big guns" chapter because there's so much information to cover. Remember, Wicca takes its practices from a variety of ancient and modern sources to make its own complete system. Because of all the material coming in from so many different places, entire books have been written about every single core topic we're going to discuss here. I've tried to give you just the core of what you need to know about each of these topics, along with some practices to put them in place.

The Wheel of the Year

If you've been worried about not having your favorite holidays to celebrate anymore by becoming Wiccan, this will be great news for you! Wicca has a complete system of eight main holidays spread evenly throughout the year. The holidays are called sabbats, coming from a French word meaning "to frolic" or "to celebrate." Each sabbat plays a special role in the lifecycles of the Goddess and God and in the birth and rebirth of nature. When you put them all together, they tell a story of how the God is born, grows up with the Goddess, and dies. Wait, the gods die? Sure they do! But they also come back to life, just like nature does. That's why we call it the wheel of the year. It's a cycle that happens every year and will continue to do so until we're not here anymore.

Each sabbat has its origin in several different ancient cultures. Mostly, the four sabbats that make up the two solstices and two equinoxes come from Northern Europe. The other four (which some people call the greater sabbats) come from the British Isles, the home of the ancient Celts. In the back of the book, you'll find a chapter with sample rituals you can do to celebrate each of the sabbats.

Yule – on or around December 21

Yule is the winter solstice and its where some consider to be the "start" of the wheel of the year (although, since it's a wheel it doesn't really have a starting or ending point). In the Wiccan mythos, this is when the God is born from the Goddess as mother. On the winter solstice, the days grow longer as the sun stays out longer in the northern hemisphere. Since the sun represents the God, the sabbat days are mostly focused on the journey of the sun as the God.

Yule is a time of warm celebration focused on family and close friends. Most of the symbols and traditions of Christmas come from the celebrations of Yule in some form or another and a Wiccan Yule celebration will often look exactly the same as a Christmas party. The practice of putting up a tree was an act of tree magick. The fir tree doesn't die in the winter so it was believed that by bringing one indoors, you could scare away the dark spirits of disease and death. Putting ornaments on the tree is simply decorating a tree with charms designed to bring your family health and prosperity. The glowing lights on the tree represent the new sun being born.

Wiccans celebrate Yule by reenacting the birth of the sun. Solitary Wiccans will usually do this by lighting a single candle at sunrise and thinking about the new things they'd like to bring into their lives for the coming year. Covens will light up bonfires to welcome in the return of the light. Lighting bonfires is a big theme in many of the sabbats and could be one of the oldest ways to celebrate the passage of the Sun God that we know of.

Imbolc – February 2

You might also hear Imbolc called Candlemas, although that's the Christianized version of this mysterious sabbat. Imbolc means "ewe's milk" since at this time, the lambs would be lactating to feed their young. It's one of those greater sabbats that we have the British Isles to thank for. The start of February is technically the middle of the winter season and in my area of the eastern United States, it's the coldest time of year. But despite the chilling weather, this sabbat is all about warmth. Warmth of the home and everyone within it. You know it's Imbolc when the days are noticeably growing in length and the very first signs of spring start to appear. Early flowers like lilies and daffodils pop up from the snowy ground and we begin to see the stirrings of spring ahead.

In the journey of the God, we find a young boy still under the care and supervision of the young Goddess. Imbolc is a unique sabbat because there's one goddess in particular that gets special attention on this day. Brigit, the Irish goddess of smithcraft, poetry, and healing is the star of the show on Imbolc. In her lore, Brigit is famous for traveling the countryside, healing the sick and feeding the hungry. This lore carried over into the Christian era when they adopted her as St. Brigit. Brigit as goddess and saint are nearly identical, showing just how important she was (and still is) to the Celtic nations.

Wiccans celebrate Imbolc by lighting up the home fireplace (if there is one) or lighting candles in all the windows of the home. Other than the spiritual significance, lighting fires and candles is just a good idea at this time of year anyway. It's the coldest month for many people so the idea of staying inside by a roaring fire is the perfect way to celebrate this turning point in the winter season. My own coven celebrates by making our own candles out of herbs and oils that correspond to the season.

Ostara – on or around March 21

Ostara is the spring equinox, the very first day of the spring season. The name Ostara comes from the name of the German goddess of spring, also called Eostre. Eostre sort of sounds like Easter, doesn't it? That's because it is! Just like Yule and Christmas, Ostara and Easter celebrations look very similar to each other.

The God is a young man at this stage, showing an interest in other young gods in his search for love. This makes Ostara a happy time with bright colors, music, and outdoor activities. It's mating season for many types of animals at this time of year, which means fertility is the trademark theme of Ostara. Eggs and rabbits are both ancient symbols of fertility associated with gods. The importance of this time was so strong that these obviously Pagan themes easily worked their way into the modern Christian celebrations of Easter. It's funny to think of Easter as an ancient Pagan fertility festival, but it's really a great way to describe it when you look at all the symbols it incorporates.

Wiccans celebrate Ostara in similar ways to Easter. Painting eggs with your wishes and dreams for the season is a common and old practice. There are a bunch of really fun modern adaptions to this practice too. Since I'm opposed to the cruelty involved in the modern egg industry, I like to get those little plastic eggs from the supermarket and fill them with spell scrolls and special herbs. I hang those on the tree outside my house and let them work their magick as they dangle in the wind. A cool decoration and a convenient way to work some magick in public without anyone noticing.

Beltane – May 1

Out of all eight sabbats on the wheel of the year, there are two that are considered to be especially important. Beltane is one of them. An extremely old fire festival from the British Isles, Beltane is known for the lighting of bonfires across the hills of the countryside. Young men and women would leap over the fires for blessings in the year and farmers would steer their cattle in between two fires to protect the herd from predators. It's one of those sabbats that have such a long and detailed history, it would be impossible to talk about it in length without giving it its own book.

The ancient Celts didn't have four seasons like we do today. Instead, they had only summer and winter. Beltane is considered the start of "summer" with the blooming of the native hawthorn tree. It was (and still is) a huge celebration across many areas with feasting, dancing, and games. One game in particular that you may have seen before is the dance of the Maypole. A pole is erected with strands of colored ribbon tied to the top. Children grab the ends of the ribbons and dance around, half going clockwise and the other half going counterclockwise. The pole represents the God and the weaving of the ribbons represents the Goddess.

In the journey of the God, he's now been married to the Goddess as Queen of the Earth. Through their love, nature springs up anew all around them, just like in the Wiccan creation myth at the start of our planet. We might think of Beltane as a sort of Wiccan Valentine's Day. Beltane is a day to spend with someone you love or admire. The tradition of giving a basket filled with gifts and signs of your affection look similar to the giving of Valentine's gifts and are a reminder that showing you care for someone is a beautiful act that can bring us closer to the gods.

Other than dancing the Maypole, Beltane is a popular time to spend in nature and do outdoor activities like hiking and camping. In the United Stated, Beltane marks the start of the Pagan festival season when big groups of Wiccans and Pagans from all over the country gather to celebrate the approaching summer. And just like ancient times, we light fires to celebrate the love of the gods for humanity.

Litha – on or around June 21

Although the ancient Celts might have thought of Beltane as the start of summer, the actual start of summer starts on Litha. Litha is one of the many names for the summer solstice and has grown into one of the most popular sabbats. This is probably because of the rise of the Pagan festivals across the US and the UK. June is an awesome time to meet other Pagans and celebrate the height of the sun. The first Pagan festival I went to was Pagan Spirit Gathering in the Midwestern area of the United States. Organized by Rev. Selena Fox, the festival is the largest of its kind and really mimics what an ancient Pagan civilization might have looked like during the start of the summer season.

There's a lot of evidence to suggest that the summer solstice was celebrated by many ancient cultures all over the world. Stonehenge in England is the most famous example of ancient solar celebrations. As the sun sets on Litha, it creates a pathway of sunlight that flows through the inner circle. Scholars haven't proven exactly why the ancient people made such a massive monument, but many people believe it was designed to mark the two solstices.

The God is at the full height of his power on Litha. He's fully grown, just as the sun has reached the height of its journey over Earth. Wiccans celebrate Litha with bonfires (as you can see, we sure do love fire!) and working magick for goals. Wiccan lore suggests that magick performed on Litha is strengthened more than any other time. We take advantage of that opportunity by working spells to secure our health and happiness for the rest of the year.

It's unlikely that many teens will be able to attend Pagan festivals since many of them are adult-only for safety reasons. But have no fear! There are still a ton of easy ways that solitary

Wiccans can share in the powerful energy of Litha. Write your desires on slips of paper and burn them, pray for dreams of the future before bedtime, or make a juice toast to the sun at noon. I've included a simply solitary ritual you can do for this sabbat (and all the sabbats) in the rituals section of this book.

Lughnassadh – August 2

Here's the sabbat with the funny name that's nearly impossible to spell. It took me years to remember how to spell Lughnassadh correctly. It turns out, there are a bunch of ways to spell it anyway. Lughnassadh, Lughnasah, and Lughnassad are all correct. Darn those Celtic languages and their extra consonants. Anyway, if Lughnassadh is too much of a tongue twister, you can always use the Catholicized version – Lammas.

Lughnassadh's key words are work and play. Two words that sound very opposite but have similar meanings for this interesting sabbat. Lughnassadh in ancient times is when the first of the crops would come in for the season. Early crops like grains would be pulled in to make way for the rest of the harvesting work ahead in the fall. Ritually, the last bunch of wheat would be cut with a special knife and crafted into a dolly, representing the gifts of fertility and sacrifice.

Note the word sacrifice – it's a chilling word. But we sacrifice things all the time to get the things we want. We sacrifice our time to school so we can get a good education and go on to get a good job. We sacrifice our spare cash on the weekends so we can get out of the house and blow off some steam from a busy week. Sacrifice means giving up something special to show your gratitude and to open up to future blessings. Wiccans will often "sacrifice" a meal to the gods in celebration of the harvest days, including Lughnassadh.

The God is growing older and is preparing to sacrifice himself for the year. The God is the embodiment of the harvest and he knows that in order for nature to flourish again, he has to prepare to leave the world. But he's not gone just yet. For now, he celebrates with the Goddess and all of us as we make awesome food and play games.

Games are common in group celebrations of Lughnassadh. The name of the sabbat itself comes from the god Lugh. Lugh was a god of great skill and so games that test the body and mind are played in his honor. It's kind of like a Celtic Olympics. The Greeks weren't the only ones to play games in honor of the gods.

Besides playing games, Wiccans will take time at Lughnassadh to look at our lives from a "harvest" point of view. What are those things you've worked hard to grow since the spring that are finally coming into being. Is there a project that's finally coming to an end? Maybe there are parts of your personality that you wanted to work on that are finally working themselves out. Take stock of your accomplishments and celebrate your victories.

Mabon – on or around September 21

Ah, here's a much easier word to say than Lughnassadh! Even though the word is easier to say, some people still get Lughnassadh and Mabon mixed up. That's because Mabon is another harvest sabbat (the second of them) that has some similar imagery to the one before it. You might think of Mabon as the "main harvest" when the majority of crops are coming in for the year. Mabon is one of two sabbats that falls on an equinox. In this case it's the autumnal equinox, the first day of fall.

In the journey of the God, we find him turning into an old man. And the Goddess, growing older with him, has turned into the wise crone. He's now preparing to die as the last of the crops are harvested. There's a little bit of sadness in the air, knowing that the end of the year is on its way, but there's still so much to celebrate too.

American Wiccans today often think of Mabon as the "Pagan Thanksgivng." Food (and lots of it) is the name of the game and entire rituals are usually built around the feast itself. We celebrate the gifts of the Earth by splurging a little and eating pretty much anything we want. Mabon is not the time to count calories!

To celebrate this day on your own, you might try and make a couple of dishes by hand. Mabon is a great time for kitchen magick so you can weave positive spells for change into your food as you prepare it.

And most of all, Mabon is about giving thanks. Gratitude is so important in Wicca. It helps us develop a good relationship with the gods and helps us to appreciate the things we have and the things that are coming our way. If all you can do on Mabon is lift your head to the sky and say "thanks!", that would be just fine enough.

Samhain – October 31

As we come to the end of the wheel of the year, you'll see that I've saved the best for last! Well, it's my favorite sabbat so I might be a little biased. Although Halloween has grown into one of the most popular non-religious holiday's today, it has a much older history as a religious festival in the form of Samhain, the day the of the dead.

Samhain, and celebrations like it, is thought to be possibly the oldest formal holiday we still celebrate today. The lighting of jack-o-lanterns, dressing up in costume, and the celebration of all things spooky are all practices that date back many hundreds of years. Remember how I mentioned Beltane being one of the two most important sabbats? Samhain is the other one.

We celebrate the dead on Samhain as we honor the death of the God on the last leg of his journey. It's at this time that he travels to the world of spirit, taking with him the souls of all those who have died in the year. This isn't a frightening process, but a journey that's welcomed by those who have wandered the Earth lost and lonely, searching for a guide to help them out. In this way, the God plays the role of Lord of the Wild Hunt, giving safe passage for the dead to travel to their otherworldly destinations.

Wiccans celebrate Samhain by honoring our ancestors and our loved ones who have died in previous years. We light candles for them, tell their stories, and even have dinner with a special place at the table set just for them. Every year at my house we host a dumb supper. The dumb supper is a silent dinner where all guests stay quiet from the time they enter the house until the moment they leave. The ancestors get their own plate with food from all the dishes.

It's believed that on Samhain, the veil that separates our world and the world of the spirits wears thin. This gives us a rare opportunity to speak to our dead loved ones, tell them how much we appreciate what they brought to us in our life, and to tell them goodbye if we didn't get the chance. If you don't know anyone who's died personally (and I didn't until I was 20 years old) you can honor "all ancestors known and unknown." They'll get the message.

After Samhain, the Goddess renews herself and the God is born again at Yule. Lather, rinse, and repeat.

Celebrating the wheel of the year and each of the sabbats causes very real changes in your life. After observing the days for a whole year, you'll realize that you can adapt better to the changing seasons. Spring's allergies might not be so rough and the gloomy dark weather of early winter might not make you feel as down as it normally does. Turning the wheel of the year causes us to become part of the wheel itself.

The Ritual Circle

In case you haven't noticed, circular things are pretty common in Wicca. The wheel of the year is of course circular as are a bunch of our sacred symbols. The most important circle for a Wiccan's day-to-day practice is the ritual circle.

In ritual, Wiccans cast a circle around their space to make it sacred and special. The practice of circle casting is really old and dates back to the magicians of the medieval times. The circle has a few different purposes:

- The circle transforms everything within it, making everything "pure" for your magick. It's especially helpful for ritual performed indoors. Indoor spaces often collect all the negative energies that float off our negative thoughts and actions. Casting a circle creates a space that's free form all that junk.
- The circle protects you while you're in it. There's nothing scary or dangerous about Wicca, but raising energy (something we'll cover later) can make some beginners feel dizzy or emotionally drained. The circle protects your energy bodies so you don't feel like crud after your ritual.
- The circle helps you pass easily between the worlds. There are many different "worlds" that exist in our universe and magick becomes effective when it's worked across all of them. Doing ritual in a circle ensures that what you're doing is being heard across all the necessary planes of existence.

Most circles for one person are around 7 to 9 feet in diameter. Larger circles (for folks who like more room to move) can be up to twice the length of your body. I like larger circles when I'm on my own, but they do take more personal energy to maintain. Casting a circle is the first act of directing energy that most Wiccans learn. Before we learn how to cast a circle though, we should first practice a directing of energy.

Exercise – Directing Energy

Have you ever rubbed your hands together really fast to feel that hot tingly feeling in your blood? That's a simple form of raising energy. There are lots of ways to raise energy that we'll get into later, but the most basic and important method for all Wiccans to learn is visualization and intent.

Step 1: Take a few deep breaths and calm yourself. Clear your head of distractions and focus only on the task at hand. In your mind, state your intention, which is that you will be raising and directing personal energy.

Step 2: Feel and imagine a warm glowing light beginning in the area right above your belly. See it in your mind's eye. Yes, I'm telling you to make-believe! It helps if you close your eyes if you find it difficult to imagine with your eyes open. If you're still having trouble "seeing" the light, just know in your heart that it's there, even if you can't see it well.

Step 3: Begin to imagine that light growing brighter and becoming more intense. It's like a ball of electric fire swirling around in your body. When you feel it's gotten as bright as you can make it, feel it begin to move out from your belly and into your arms. As it moves, it lights up your arms with warmth and color. Let it continue to move as it flows into your hands.

Step 4: Hold your hands about 6 inches apart from each other, both palms facing each other. Push that light out from your physical body and into the space between your hands. Feed that light with the light of your belly, your inner being, as the light collects and becomes brighter in the air between your hands.

Step 5: Practice passing the light between both of your hands. Visualize it in different colors if you can. Try forming it into shapes like a sphere, and then into more complicated shapes like cones and cubes after you get the hang of that. When you're done, you can simply absorb the light back into your hands where it seeps back into your body.

Easy enough, right? Well, for some of you it might be easy. Visualizing can come natural to some people while others have to practice frequently to get the hang of it. I had a terrible time using visualization to direct energy at first. I did learn a little trick that helped me catch on though.

To increase your visualization skills, try staring at a simple object on a plain surface. A bright red apple on your kitchen table is a good example. Stare at the apple for a while, taking in as much detail as you can. The shape it makes, its color, its texture, and even the shadow it casts. In the middle of looking at it, shut your eyes and see if you can make that apple appear before you in your mind. Do that over and over with different objects until you can hold the image in your mind for a couple of minutes at a time.

Once you're able to direct energy in a basic way, you'll be ready to cast a basic circle. There are a few ways to cast a circle but the core of it, directing the energy, is always there. The words and physical movements are the steps that vary. In fact, you don't even have to say anything while casting the circle. But using words helps to focus our intention, making the circle that much more effective.

Exercise – Casting a Circle

Stand in the center of your space and take a few deep breaths. Feel yourself relax and become comfortable in your body. With every inhale, take in confidence and power from the air around you. That air entering you turns into light as it fills your belly, and then your entire body.

Continue to breathe until you feel you've taken in all the light from around you that you can manage. Feel the light concentrating and being directed towards your projective arm. Your projective arm has the hand you use to write with.

As you feel the energy flowing into your arm, approach the outer area of where you want the circle to be. Traditionally, you would approach the east and begin the casting there. But if you don't know where east is, don't sweat it.

Once you're at the boundary area, bring your index and pointer finger together and point them to the floor as you imagine the light from your body and the air around you flowing down into a bright line of electric fire. You might imagine it as a sort of laser beam, or even a small, highly focused flame thrower!

Walk the boundary of your circle area deosil (clockwise), continuing to pour out energy from your fingers. As the energy falls out of you and touches the ground, it rises up like a dome above you, and into the ground below you. Walk the circle three times as you form a glowing sphere of energy, with you being in the center of it. While walking the circle, you can say these words:

I conjure thee, O great circle!
Be for me a sacred grove, consecrated in the name of the Goddess and God
Let all things foul and profane fall away from this space
Let the hedge of nature's beauty spring up and keep me safe
Let the power I raise within be focused and true
Let all the worlds witness my rite and come to my aid
For thrice about the circle's bound
I stand in power between sky and ground.
As above and so below, so mote it be, I make it so!

As you say the last line, move back into the center of the circle and feel its energy pulsing all around you. Forward, behind, left, right, above and below. The phrase "so mote it be" is a common saying in Wicca and basically means "may it be so." Saying it seals what you just did and affirms it in all the worlds.

That's it! Your circle is now cast and you're ready to move on to the next steps of your ritual or whatever else you planned to do. You don't actually have to have a full ritual planned to cast a circle. When I first learned how to do it, I would cast one just to sit within it and meditate. It gave me practice and increased my confidence by doing it over and over without anything else to worry about.

Make sure that once you're inside the circle, you don't cross through it for any reason. Passing through it with your body will either severely weaken the energy, or punch a hole in it entirely. We don't want holes in our circles because the energy can leak out, rendering the circle itself useless. If you have to leave the circle for something, you can cut a door. Run your fingers downward in the air before you and imagine the energy parting like a curtain. Reverse that move when you reenter, sealing it back up again. Try to avoid that if you can though.

When you're done and ready to leave the circle, you'll need to "release" it. Releasing the circle contains the same steps as casting the circle, but with everything in reverse.

First, approach the circle in the west (again, if you don't know where west is just start at the opposite side from where you cast the circle). Point your fingers down and begin to walk the circle boundary in the widdershins (counterclockwise) direction.

As you walk, visualize the energy from the sphere flowing back into your fingers, and then back into the core of your body. Walk the boundary three times, imagining the circle's light glowing dimmer and dimmer as the energy seeps back into you. By the time you reach the west for the third time, the energy should be all gone.

Step back into the center and affirm the release of the circle with these words:

Thrice about the circle's unbound
as excess light returns to the ground
As above so below – the circle is open, but unbroken
Merry meet, merry part, and merry meet again.
So mote it be.

The language in the circle releasing helps to ground down any extra energies flying about that might have escaped your grasp while walking the circle. If you still feel like there's a lot of energy buzzing about the space, splash some cool water on your face or have a bite to eat. You shouldn't feel spacey after that.

The Guardians

In the more formal of rituals within Wicca, there's a practice in setting up a space that comes after casting the circle. There's a few names for the practice but usually you'll hear it as "calling the guardians," "calling the quarters," or "invoking the watchers." They're all correct and essentially the same. Wiccans like to use different names for the same thing, as we saw when learning about the sabbats.

The guardians (there are four of them) are beings stationed at each of the four directions. The practice of calling them into a circle mostly comes from the ceremonial magick of Dr. John Dee in his Enochian system. We also see the guardians in an Italian tradition of witchcraft called Stregha. The Stregha call the guardians "Grigori" and they play an important role in protecting the crafter while they work their rituals.

The guardians are called after the circle is cast and they're each called individually, starting in the east and ending in the north. The guardians are said to reside in "watchtowers" or stations that contain all the powers they bring to the world. Usually each guardian is called along with their corresponding element. To incorporate calling the four guardians, you can use the outline below.

Exercise – Calling the Guardians

Face east and raise your arms in the air before you like you're doing the first move in the *YMCA* dance. Draw in your first big breath and speak the words of calling. Many Wiccans prefer to make up their own calls but for the purpose of starting out, you can use these sample calls:

Guardian of the east, spirits of air
come to me from your mighty watchtowers
and bless my rite with insight and inspiration
Be with me and ward this place as I work my rite
Guardians of the east, hail and welcome!

Imagine the guardian of the east stepping forward in whatever form you like. I like to imagine the guardians as being without gender, although some Wiccan traditions identify the east and south guardians as male and the west and north guardians as female. I think the guardians are so old and all-encompassing that they're without gender, but do whatever feels right for you.

I also like to imagine the element mentioned in the call flowing into the circle. The quarter calls are dual-purpose because you're calling the element that the guardian rules over as well. For the east, I might imagine gusts of wind blowing into the circle. Do the same for the other directions as well. Fire entering into the south, the waves of the ocean entering in the west, and dark soil from the Earth falling into place from the north.

Next, move clockwise to the south, again raising your arms. Call out to the guardian of the south:

Guardian of the south, spirits of fire
come to me from your mighty watchtowers
and bless my rite with passion and purpose
Be with me and ward this place as I work my rite
Guardians of the south, hail and welcome!

Move again to your right and call out to the guardian of the west:

Guardian of the west, spirits of water
come to me from your mighty watchtowers
and bless my rite with rhythm and grace
Be with me and ward this place as I work my rite

Guardians of the west, hail and welcome!

Finally, make one last turn as you raise your arms to the north and say:

Guardian of the north, spirits of earth
come to me from your mighty watchtowers
and bless my rite with honor and strength
Be with me and ward this place as I work my rite
Guardians of the north, hail and welcome!

And that's all there is to it. When you're done with your ritual, you'll want to bid farewell to each guardian in reverse before you leave the circle. You would start at the north and work counter clockwise, saying words like this for each direction:

Guardian of the [direction], spirits of [element]
thank you for joining me in this rite
Go if you must but stay if you like
Hail and farewell!

Always acknowledge the guardians after your ritual is over if you called them. Otherwise, they might just crash at your place until you let them know they're not needed any longer. And trust me, it's not fun trying to get to sleep when the southern guardian is still flinging fire energies all over the place.

The Elements

The four classical elements are the rock stars of Wicca. We incorporate them in some form or another in just about everything we do. One or more of the elements can be found in every single sabbat, quarter call, ritual tool, and spell. Since Wicca is a nature-based religion, it makes sense that the building blocks of nature would make up the base of all our practices.

Of course, if you've already studied high-school biology you know from the periodic table that there are more than four elements. The elements Wicca and most other nature-based practices speak of are the four classical elements: earth, air, fire, and water. We have the ancient Greek philosophers to thank for giving us this neat little elemental system.

Everything in nature contains at least one element, including our own bodies. Everything from the water in our skin to the earth of our bones to the iron flecks that float through our blood are comprised of the elements. Even modern inventions like computers and cars all run off the elements in some way.

The goal of the Wiccan is to commune with the four elements as much as possible. By moving in harmony with them, we step into their gentle rhythm and receive all the wisdom they have to offer. These wisdoms are extremely valuable to Wiccans as we're constantly seeking to live in a way that's more mindful of our place in the world.

Remember that everything in nature has a correspondence, something that relates it to something else. Learning about each element and its correspondences is important for our rituals, devotional practices, and especially magick. There are so many correspondences for each element, so here's a quick guide to some of the main ones.

Air

Direction: east
Colors: yellow or white
Tool: wand
Animals: birds
Creature: Sylph
Powers: beginnings, inspiration, insight, communication, intelligence
Planets: Mercury, Neptune
Astrological signs: Gemini, Libra, Aquarius

Day of the week: Wednesday
Season: spring

Fire

Direction: south
Colors: red or orange
Tool: athame
Animals: cats, lizards, fireflies
Creature: Drake
Powers: passion, success, protection, courage
Planets: sun, Mars
Astrological signs: Aries, Leo, Sagittarius
Days of the week: Sunday, Tuesday
Season: summer

Water

Direction: west
Colors: blue, silver
Tool: chalice
Animals: fish, seagulls, cranes
Creature: Undine
Powers: intuition, psychism, compassion, transformation
Planets: moon, Venus
Astrological signs: Cancer, Scorpio, Pieces
Days of the week: Monday, Friday
Season: fall

Earth

Direction: north
Colors: brown, black, green
Tool: peyton (altar pentacle)
Animals: Most four-legged animals that live within the Earth.
Especially bears, groundhogs and prairie dogs
Creature: Gnome

Powers: stability, knowledge, prosperity, growth
Planets: Jupiter, Saturn, Earth
Astrological signs: Taurus, Virgo, Capricorn
Days of the week: Thursday, Saturday
Season: winter

Using the elemental correspondences, there are a lot of ways we can tap into each element. Matching up as many correspondences as possible when attuning to the elements is a method Wiccans use to stand in the greatest flow of power possible. Although magick can be performed anywhere, it helps to know about which elemental correspondences will give you a hand. Magick and all spiritual power follows the path of least resistance, so make it easy for the power to come your way.

Exercise – Attuning to the Elements

Attunement is the act of matching up your own personal energies with the energies of something else. Everything on the planet (and outside of our planet) is constantly vibrating with energy. Learning to sync yourself up with the elements is an important part of developing a strong nature-based spirituality.

To start, pick an element and prepare yourself with as many correspondences to that element that you can incorporate. For example, if I'm attuning to earth I might wear brown and green clothes, light a green candle, and have a picture of an earth animal before me. I might also schedule my attunement to be on a Thursday or a Saturday. You get the picture...

Sit comfortably, back straight, and breathe deeply. As you breathe, allow any other thoughts besides the act of breathing pass you by. Begin to think of the element you want to attune yourself with.

With your mind's eye, "see" the element clearly. What is the first thing you think of when you begin to think about that element? For me, my first thoughts on earth usually lead me to a dark and lush forest, alive with many different types of animals and plants. For you it might be a cave, a mountain range, or your favorite type of stone. It could be that tree you like to read under in the park. Whatever the image is, see it with as much detail as your mind can conjure up.

Once you have a good image in place, engage your other senses. What does that element smell like in the form you're visualizing? What does it feel like? Is it hot or cold? Wet or dry? Does it have a sound, or maybe a combination of a few different sounds? Immerse yourself completely within that scene.

With your hand, trace an invoking pentacle before you. The five points of the pentacle represent the four elements plus the spirit of the divine. Invoking pentacles draw in power and are traced widdershins (counterclockwise). So start at the top point of the star and trace downwards towards the bottom-left. Then continue to the right point, then the left, then to the bottom-right, and return back to the top.

Complete the pentacle by tracing the widdershins circle around the points. If you like, you can trace the invoking pentacle in a color of energy that corresponds to the element you're calling.

Imagine the invoking pentacle hovering in the air before you as you call the element forth from the star to swirl around your body. You can either visualize this process on its own, or combine it with the invocations below:

Air:
Come to me air, breath of the sky
gift of the birds and song of the wind

Fire:
Come to me fire, flame of my heart
heat of the sun and passion strong

Water:

> *Come to me water, spiraling waves*
> *movement of rivers, compassion unending*

Earth:

> *Come to me earth, depths of cave*
> *strong standing stones, my stable foundation*

Continue to feel the power of the element flow out of the pentacle like a portal. Let it mingle with your body, mind, and heart. Notice how it makes you feel and what emotions it triggers. When you're done, feel the element flowing back into the pentacle. Then "erase" the pentacle in the air with your hand, like you're wiping it away.

When I first learned methods of communing with the elements, these exercises of visualizing each one and having them encircle my body were my favorite. The more I practiced, the more I could physically feel the effects of each elements in my own personal space. That's not to say you'll end up having a waterfall appear in your room, but you might get a cooling sensation, like chilled mist blowing on your face. Fire is usually the most noticeable. I've been to many rituals where calling fire immediately makes the room feel warmer. The elements are real, physical things, so don't be surprised when they get physical with you!

Exercise – Elemental Blessing

Here's another exercise that calls upon the elements to enter your space. The difference here is that you're not only calling each element to join you, but you're doing so with an intention. In this case, the intention is to bless a person, space, or object.

Blessing with the elements is a long and beloved practice in Wicca that you just never stop doing. I cleanse and bless objects and my home just as often as I did when I first started. I love this practice because it's an easy way of incorporating the elements in their physical form, which is always best if you can make it happen.

Let's start with a physical object. For example, you might want to bless a necklace to give you peace and protection when you wear it. The necklace will become a physical container, anchoring the power of each element in this world for you. With a blessed necklace, you could easily call upon each element to be with you in a flash.

Materials:

A representation of air (feathers or incense)
A representation of fire (a lit candle is best, or you could use a powered-on lamp if you can't use flame)
A representation of water (a cup of water should be pretty easy to obtain)
A representation of earth (dirt or salt is best for this)
Object to be blessed
Take up your object in one hand and your "air" in the other. Use your feather or the smoke of the incense to waft the element across the object. As you do this, say:

I summon, stir, and conjure thee oh spirits of air
bless this [object] and infuse it with your love.
Blessed be, spirits of air

Wave the object over the flame or around the light bulb (carefully!). Imagine flames flowing into the object as you say:

I summon, stir, and conjure thee oh spirits of fire
bless this [object] and infuse it with your love.
Blessed be, spirits of fire

Dip the object into the cup of water. If it's too big (or you're blessing a person or room) just sprinkle it with your fingers. Imagine powerful waves crashing into the object, imbuing it with all the mysteries of the sea. Again, say:

I summon, stir, and conjure thee oh spirits of water
bless this [object] and infuse it with your love.
Blessed be, spirits of water

Finally, take up the dirt or salt and slowly sprinkle it across the object. If it's small enough, you might even bury it inside a bowl of it and roll it around with your fingers. As you do so, imagine dark vines creeping up from the Earth and encircling the object. Call out to earth:

I summon, stir, and conjure thee oh spirits of earth
bless this [object] and infuse it with your love.
Blessed be, spirits of earth

Congratulations, you just performed your first elemental blessing! Pretty easy, right? Easy but incredibly powerful and effective. But don't forget to thank your elemental buddies for the assistance! Raise your arms up and call out to all the elements at once:

Oh great elementals,
spirits of the earth, the air, the fire, and the water
I thank you for powers and blessings
be with me in peace and may you be forever blessed.
So mote it be!

Spirit – the Fifth Element

While we're on the topic of the elements, we can't forget about spirit. Although spirit is considered to be within all the elements, it's an element all on its own in most traditions of Wicca. Think of spirit as all those non-physical things that you know are present, but can't physically touch. Love, compassion, gratitude, confidence, family, pride, joy, and wholeness are all feelings commonly described as manifestations of spirit.

Remember that in the Wiccan creation myth, the gods emerged from the void as pure energy, without form or purpose. That's the origin of spirit. In the Eastern parts of the world they call it qi or akasha, the invisible force that animates all forms of life. When you passed the energy from hand to hand and shaped it into different forms, you were working with spirit.

Spirit has its own point on the five points of the pentacle because all other elements need it to survive. Each element could not it exist if it weren't for the mysterious spark of life that gives it the energy it needs to exist in the world. The funny thing about spirit is that even though it's not of this world, its present within all things in this world.

Through spirit, we learn that all things on this planet have their own purpose, their own importance. We learn that all things are valuable and worthy in the eyes of the divine because all things are formed of divine energy. Honoring spirit as an element reminds us that we are all made of stars.

Tools - Getting and Using Wiccan Gear

Wicca is a very hands-on religion and our huge number of tools really drive that point home. Most people who follow Pagan paths today really love their gear. I'll definitely admit to counting myself among them. Tools are just fun. They give us something tangible to look at, focus on, and hold in our hands. Sure we can use our fingers to cast the circle, but there's nothing like the grip of a wand in your hand to get you pumped for ritual.

Tools have always been an important part of Wicca. We get most of our tools from the ceremonial practitioners who got their information from the medieval magicians. The cool thing about tools is that they're one of the few aspects of Wicca that retains a very old history without ever having changed all that much. Progress is great, but it's nice to have things that connect us to that romantic past of the magick of old.

Most of the longtime Wiccans I know have a bunch of tools – probably too many. I'm guilty of that. In fact, I have an entire room in my house devoted to storing all my gear. It's kind of ridiculous actually. But, I have lots of gear because it's fun and I've learned how to work my Wicca without necessarily needing any of it (but more on that later).

The core tools in Wicca all have specific jobs that they perform in ritual and acts of magick. Each one represents a part of our magickal personalities. Since they're tied to us, they're not effective unless *we* are effective. Tools are only as powerful as the Wiccan is without them. Make sense? Let me put it another way. My first high priestess Miss Shannon used to tell me this when I would worry myself about having the right tools:

"In Wicca, tools are just the icing on the cake. There's no point in having 'stuff' if you haven't got the stuff inside to make them work."

That said, let's take a look at the core tools Wiccans use and what each one is for.

A Wiccan altar with tools.

Athame

The athame (usually pronounced like atha-may) is a knife, usually double-edged and with a black handle, that's used for directing magickal energy. In any of the exercises you've already learned where two fingers are used to direct energy, the athame could be used instead. The athame comes straight from the magickal books of the medieval magicians who would use the athame to cast their very complicated circles for spirit conjuration.

In modern Wicca, the athame is a catch-all tool that's used for pretty much all of our energy direction needs.

Traditionally, the handle is black because the color black attracts and absorbs energy from the atmosphere around it. Think of it like a psychic battery. That's also the reason why in some Wiccan traditions, practitioners wear black robes for rituals.

Why use a blade to direct energy, rather than something else with a black handle? The blade of the knife is important because it represents our will that we're putting forth with our energy. A knife needs to be sharp to cut anything effectively and so too must our will be sharp and keen to cause any real change.

Practically, the tip of the blade acts as a focal point to make the direction of our energy more precise. It's like turning a flashlight beam into a laser. The metal blade is forged with heat, making the athame the elemental tool of fire.

I got lucky with my first athame. In the year I started practicing Wicca, we moved into a new house and the previous owners had left all sorts of junk in the attic and garage. While helping my mother sift through it all, I came across a double-edged dagger with a black handle. The handle had some kind of sculpted spider on it. Not only had I found a perfect athame, but I'm still pretty sure that's exactly what it was made to be!

It's unlikely that you'll randomly stumble across an athame of your own in your house and most companies won't sell knives to those under 18 in most states. But have no fear, we can improvise!

Any knife can be used as an athame in a pinch. In fact, it's more likely that the old cunning witches during the Middle Ages would use a kitchen knife rather than a ceremonial-looking dagger. The kitchen knife wouldn't draw unwanted attention and could be hidden amongst everything else in the kitchen.

If you can, use a sharp cutting knife from your own kitchen. You should also be able to buy a cheap one of your own for a pretty low price at a home-supply store. If neither option is possible, a butter knife will do. And if you can, try painting the bottom of the handle black with paint. I once saw a teen I know paint the handle with black fingernail polish. Brilliant! Wicca is an innovative practice, so don't be afraid to get creative and do whatever works.

You can also decorate it further by painting or carving your name and some magickal symbols into the handle and blade. The ancient books of magick like the Key of Solomon have all kinds of fancy instructions on exactly what kind of symbols to paint on the blade. Whatever you do with it, make it feel like something that's an extension of your own body.

Use the athame as you would for anything your fingers could do. So far we've learned how to cast a circle and draw the invoking pentacle of the elements. Try those exercises with your athame. Over time, the knife will store more and more energy, making it that much more effective.

There's one major rule with the athame though. It should never cut anything physical, ever. Many traditions are so strict about this that even the act of cutting something with the athame on accident means the practitioner must immediately bury and abandon it. Others say it's okay, as long as its thoroughly cleansed and rededicated.

Wand

Here's something from the land of witchcraft make-believe that's

100% real to modern Wiccans. Although it can't be used to knock out walls or paralyze your enemies, the wand has a long and important history in magickal practice.

The wand has functions very similar to the athame. It's another tool to direct energy, although the energy it directs can be a little different. The athame is a tool of fire, a symbol of our cunning will. The wand is a tool of air, a symbol of our intellect and mind.

I like to use the wand when energy is being sent for a spell. Spells can be tricky and require a big part of our mental abilities to make them stick. Sending spell energy with a wand helps to "seal" it across all the worlds. Think of it this way: the wand could be used to direct energy outside of your space, while the athame is used to direct energy inside your space. Of course, there are many Wiccans who use the wand for all the functions of the athame as well, since they just prefer it.

For the teen, a wand in place of an athame altogether is usually a better option. It's extremely easy to make one and it won't make anyone in your house nervous, like a knife might. After all, the wand is essentially just a stick that you're programming with magickal intent. Easy enough.

Most wands are made of wood that's been ritually cut from a tree or picked up from around the base of one. Wiccan shops sell gorgeous wands from other materials like clay, copper, and even gold. Even though I love my shiny tools, my wand is about as basic as they come, a sanded branch from a black walnut tree. Making your own wand is easy and will be one of your most rewarding memories on your Wiccan journey.

Crafting a Wand

First, you need to select the tree you want your wand to come from. Do some research on the trees in your area and find one that matches the kind of energy you want it to have. Every type of tree has its own unique personality and energy type. Here's a short list of some trees native to North America and some of their correspondences:

Alder – Spiritual guidance, bravery
Apple – Love, beauty, connection to the Goddess
Ash – Mental power, growing skills, justice
Beech – Seeing the past and future, ancestors
Birch – Healing, cleansing, patience, renewal
Cedar – Cleansing, preservation, and harmony
Cherry – High energy, focus, joy, mental clarity
Elder – Banishment, wisdom, calling spirit allies, beloved by faeries
Elm – Transformation, opens gateways, beloved by the faeries
Hawthorn – Psychic power, courage, wisdom, connection to the God
Hazel – Creativity, communication, and air-magick. Beloved by the Celts for making wands
Hickory – Attraction, influence, forceful change
Holly – Dream-magick, protection, physical strength
Maple – Friendship, intellect, abundance, movement
Myrtle – Introspection, honesty, truth
Oak – Power, skill, and strength of all kinds. A popular wood for wands today
Pine – Endurance, life, purification
Poplar – Enhances magickal goals, brings hope in difficult situations
Reed – Courage, destiny, fate
Rowan – Freedom, guidance, understanding
Walnut, Black – Astral travel, encouragement, weather-magick
Willow – Crone goddesses, healing, emotion, moon-magick, divination
Yew – Otherworld travel, binding, removing obstacles

There might also be a particular tree you're attracted to in your yard or your favorite park. In that case, the type of tree doesn't matter as much as your connection with it. If you feel very drawn to the willow tree in your yard but aren't interested in working with the crone goddess, that's okay!

Approach your tree of choice and sit underneath it. Meditate for a while and have a conversation with the tree in your mind. Let it know of your intentions and what you plan to do. Eventually, ask it for permission to take one of its branches. Usually as long as you approach the tree with good intentions, you'll feel a "yes" answer. If you feel overcome with a strong feeling against taking from that tree, abandon your quest for at least a month before you try again.

If you get an affirmative answer, touch the branch that you plan to take. Tell it that you wish for the vitality of the tree to leave this part of the branch, but that you wish for its powers to remain. This will limit the amount of harm that comes to the tree. Still, take only what you need and no more. Some say it's best to cut a wand during the winter, when the spirit of the tree has gone dormant for the year.

Cut the branch off and wrap it in cloth, taking care that it doesn't touch the ground before you bring it home. Common wand-lore states that letting a wand touch the bare ground encourages the power of the wood to return back to the Earth. I could never find a historical argument to back this up, so it's not something I pay much attention to.

Once you have the branch, cut it to length. The average wand would be the length from your elbow to the tip of your middle finger. I like my wands to be a little shorter so do whatever feels comfortable. After making the cuts, leave it indoors to dry for at least one month, preferably three if you have the patience for it.

After the drying time, cast a circle and bless the wand with the elements. Now it's ready for use! Just like the athame, it will grow in strength the longer you use it. Since it's a tool of the mind, it will "learn" about you over the years. The more it knows about you, the more effective it becomes in directing your energy.

Chalice

Chalice, goblet, and cup are all names for the elemental tool of water. The chalice has strong and ancient symbolism to Pagans of all paths. Its magickal lore even extends to Christianity where we find the lore of the Holy Grail, the magickal cup that Christ was said to have drunk from during the last supper.

In Wicca, the chalice represents the womb of the Goddess and all the regenerative powers of the divine feminine. Because of this, it's a healing symbol and a tool for transformation and internal change. Wiccans use the chalice to drink special potions for personal transformation and to pour out libations, liquid offerings to the gods.

A major ritual in Wicca is called the Great Rite, a mimicking of the sexual union of the Goddess and God. To reenact this, a practitioner will plunge the athame (representing the God) into the chalice. The act symbolizes the powers of creation and draws the joy of the universe into the circle.

The chalice has symbolism very similar to its larger cousin, the cauldron. Any cup can be used as a chalice, although stemmed wine glasses and goblets are the norm.

Cauldron

Ah, the old Halloween image of the frightening hag stirring a massive bubbling cauldron. The image has been linked with witchcraft since ancient times and judging by the popular image of witches around Halloween, it's not going anywhere anytime soon.

Like the athame, the cauldron was a practical tool for the witches of old. Big suppers would be made in these big cast-iron pots that could feed a whole family for days. Kitchen witches keep the old tradition of saying spells of health and protection over the family meals while they cook on the stove.

There are several goddesses associated with the cauldron as a tool for magickal transformation. The most famous story is of the goddess Cerridwen that we read about briefly in the chapter on the gods. It represents the void that the Goddess first emerged from in the creation myth. It's symbolic of the caves where early humans took shelter and where later prophets and magick-workers would gather for their rites. Its deep belly and ability to make water look black when full represents the mystery of the witch's craft and the deep well of power we draw from in our practices.

In ritual, the cauldron is used for all sorts of things that the chalice isn't big enough to do. Filling up a cauldron with water and staring into the depths of it can bring visions of the past and future. Unique to the cauldron is its function as a burning receptacle. On the full moon, write your wishes on slips of paper and burn them inside the cauldron. It is said as they transform into ash, the situation is being transformed from imagination to reality.

The cauldron was probably the last of the big tools I was able to get. They're not very easy to come by unless you have access to a Wiccan supply shop locally or online. I've had friends who had luck finding them at Army-Navy stores or second-hand camping outlets. If you still don't have any luck finding a traditional-looking cauldron, you can always use a deep pot with a black inside.

Exercise – Cauldron Meditation

The cauldron meditation is wonderfully calming to the mind and body. It brings you to a place of stillness when you might have a lot of busy thoughts flying around your brain. Having a calm mind will enable you to focus your energy better and allow you to get into a relaxed state when you're outside of a ritual setting. It's a method of training the mind that will give lasting benefits, inside the circle and out.

The cauldron meditation is easy to set up but takes a bit of continued practice before you can begin to feel the long-lasting effects. Simply fill up your cauldron (or bowl, or pot) to the very top with water. Set it before you in a dark space, but with just enough light to see it in front of you. I like doing this in a darkened room with one candle, a few feet behind me.

Stare into the surface of the water and relax your mind. Take long soothing breaths and let yourself fall into a state of deep relaxation. If you're looking at your reflection, allow your gaze to soften by unfocusing your eyes. Relax them so they're looking inside the cauldron, but not concerned with the details of what's in it.

Continue to softly stare within the water as you feel your consciousness falling into the depths of the cauldron. Feel the dark water enclosing all around you, warm and calming. Feel the comfort of being supported by the waters on all sides, like a baby in the womb. If any thoughts pop up, acknowledge them for a second and let them move on. When you feel like you're in a place of total oneness and connection with the inner depths of the cauldron, you know it's working well.

Once you're done, sharpen the focus of your eyes and pull your consciousness up from the depths of the cauldron. Dump out the water and stretch, to return fully to your waking mind.

Besom

The last of our Hollywood-style witch gear is the besom, the witch's broom. The image of witches flying around on broomsticks isn't a new one. If you take a look at the woodcut drawings of the European witch trials, you'll see images of women and men flying across the sky with various animal familiars at their side.

Of course, witches can't really fly physically through the air (man don't I wish I could!). What we can do with the broom is really amazing though. The besom is one of the air tools and has the power to sweep away any nasty energy in our space. It's the ultimate magickal cleansing tool. Simply hold the besom on the side of your body that has your dominant hand. From forward to back, sweep the air above the floor. You can actually sweep the floor if you like, but many Wiccans prefer to just sweep the air to keep the besom in the best physical condition.

Its other function is to help "fly" (in meditation) to the other realms to receive information from your spirit guides and gods. This is more of an advanced practice used in traditional witch-craft which they call hedge-riding. The hedge in this case is the veil that separates the physical human world from the world of spirit. This type of otherworld travel is similar to one of the functions of the circle, except you're going to the otherworld rather than bringing the otherworld to you. Hedge-riders believe this can result in more memorable experiences.

Traditional besoms are made with specific types of wood and plant matter and look a lot like what you'd see a movie or TV witch carrying around. Other than Wiccan supply shops or the internet, some of the best places to find these are at Renaissance festivals or medieval reenactment fairs.

If you can't find one there, you could get your own kitchen broom and bless it with the elements. The besom is considered more of a secondary, nonessential tool and I know a lot of Wiccans who don't bother using one at all. There are many ways to cleanse a space and visit the other worlds.

Peyton

You should know that not a lot of non-Gardnerian Wiccans call this tool a peyton anymore, but I still think it's a helpful word to use. The peyton is a physical pentacle that you keep on your altar, either in the center of it or towards the top. You'll also simply hear it called an "altar pentacle."

The peyton represents either the element of earth on the altar, or acts as a representation of all the elements and spirit combined. It's usually made of stone or some kind of metal. Again, these are hard to come by unless you buy one from a Wiccan supplier or make your own. My first peyton was a sheet of paper that I drew a pentacle on and laminated three times to make it firm. Hey, whatever works!

Wiccans use the peyton to bless other things used for ritual. In the sharing of cakes and drink, a common practice in coven ritual, the food is placed on the peyton and blessed with the athame. You can also hold it in your hands before you and use it as a focal point when calling the elements, especially earth.

Book of Shadows

Last but not least in our list of tools is the book of shadows. We learned a little about the book in the chapter about the early Gardnerian Wiccans. In those days, there was a single book that every initiate had to hand copy, with little to no variation at all. These days, the book is meant to be a living, changing document, personal to every practitioner.

The book of shadows can be thought of as a magickal journal and recipe book. Although the things that go into it vary depending on the person, they usually contain spells, rituals, lore, correspondences, and the outcome of spells cast.

Many Wiccans consider the book of shadows to be one of the most important tools. It's important because it not only stores all our useful workings in one place, but also chronicles our spiritual journeys as we grow along our path. My first book of shadows was two gigantic spiral-bound notebooks that I attached together. Although it's in rough shape now, I still look back on it fondly as a nice reminder of where I was as a young 12-year-old Wiccan.

The book is especially useful for documenting the types of rituals and spells we've done and what happened afterwards. So if you worked a spell that didn't work out, you can go back to the details of exactly what you did and review it. If you haven't already, start your own book of shadows as soon as you can.

Hardcover journals are great because they're compact and will last you a long time. Those spiral-bound notebooks are great if you have to use one, but their pages do start to fall out eventually.

But Wait, There's More!

This chapter was just a basic snapshot of the typical things Wiccans believe and how we put those beliefs into practice. Keep in mind that Wicca also includes many spiritual and magickal practices from a variety of different traditions from all over the world. As you continue on your path, you'll come across material from different teachers and schools of thought that you'll want to incorporate into your practice. Some of it you'll keep as a permanent part of your belief system and some of it you'll toss. Remember, Wicca is about doing what works.

Moving forward, see what you can incorporate into your life right now. What's the next sabbat coming up? Check the list of sabbat days in this chapter then check out the ritual chapter at the back of the book for an easy ritual to perform around it. What kind of tools can you start incorporating? How's that altar coming along?

In the next chapter, we'll take Wiccan beliefs a little further and start learning how to put more of them into practice.

Chapter 4

Ritual

In case you haven't noticed so far, ritual is very important in Wicca. It's so important that nearly any simple life act can be "ritualized" or infused with sacred energy and magick. There's a common joke that those who come to Wicca from Catholicism feel right at home because of all the ritual we use.

Ritual is important for many reasons that the ancient people knew well. It creates a special time for us to do something sacred. Whether that sacred thing is magick, prayer, devotionals, or rites of passage, affects the way the ritual is formed. What they all have in common is that they open up our minds to the spiritual forces at work by the gods. They speak to those inner parts of the brain and say "Hey, something different is happening here. Pay attention!" And when the mind and body are paying attention – what we call "properly prepared" – more power can flow.

Properly Prepared

Being properly prepared means that you're fit for ritual mentally, physically, and spiritually. Since most of us aren't always walking around in a perfectly balanced state, we develop some tricks and tools to help us get there for ritual. Mostly, it involves some type of cleansing for each "self."

Exercise – Cleansing the Three Selves

The first step is easy since it involves doing things you do every day. To cleanse your body physically, take a shower or bath. To make it a sacred bath, you can add salt to the water and bless it with the elements. Do the same with your food for the day and try to eat healthy foods that nourish the body if possible. Oh, and drink lots of water.

Next, cleanse the mental body. My favorite way to do this is to write a long journal entry, pouring out all the random thoughts that pop up into my head. Write down anything that enters your brain, however nonsensical it is. This is called stream-of-consciousness writing and is a great way to cleanse the mind. Besides that, getting a good night's sleep is a great way to ensure mental clarity.

Finally, cleanse the spiritual self. There are many, many ways to do that. Wiccans like to burn dried bundles of sage and wave the smoke around the body. When I was a teen this usually wasn't possible, if only for the lack of sage in my area. Now it's a little easier since many health-food stores will carry it next to the oils and incense. Still, sage might not always be practical. It does smell pretty strong so your family might not like it being burned at all. To get around this, we can do an energy cleansing that you don't need any tools for.

Stand up and begin to gather light energy into your hands as we've already learned how to do. When enough light is gathered, stretch your arms and your whole body as high up as possible, then swoop your arms down in big dramatic motions. Visualize the energy pouring over your whole body, carrying away any psychic crud that might be lurking about.

Types of Wiccan Rituals

Now that we know how to prepare for rituals of all kinds, we can look at the types of Wiccan rituals and how they relate to you. We're going to get very general here since there are literally tens of thousands of Wiccan rituals out there in print already. Luckily for us, we don't have to look at every single one. Instead, I'll break down for you the three main categories that most of them fit into:

- Sabbat/Esbat Rituals: Any ritual that celebrates a sabbat or any part of the lunar cycle. Usually these are celebration-based and revolve around the telling of stories, the sharing of food, and some type of internal reflecting process. A lot of sabbat rituals are designed to help a practitioner learn the lesson that particular sabbat brings to humanity. We look to where we are in the journey of the God. Similarly, esbat rituals help us relate our lives to the journey of the Goddess, in whatever stage she is in. Neither of these are limited to male practitioners or female practitioners. In sabbat rituals, all women can relate to the journey of the God just as all men can relate to the Goddess in the esbats.

- Rites of Passage Rituals: These are rituals designed to mark any kind of big change in a person's life, usually focused around age. The first rite of passage a family-born Wiccan would go through would be the Wiccaning – a type of baptism that blesses the newborn. There are rituals designed to mark the passage of a child into the stage of young manhood or womanhood. More obvious rites of passage would include wedding ceremonies called handfastings, divorce ceremonies called handpartings, and funeral rituals.

- Magickal Rituals: Magickal ritual is designed to be a container for spells, detailed meditations, or any other energetic working. It helps to work spells in rituals because the frame of the ritual can help the energy along and keep a spell from flopping (yes, they can do that!).

The Goals of Ritual

Besides the different types of rituals, there are also several core goals for them. All Wiccan rituals will have at least one of these goals, and many of them will have two or more.

- Altering Consciousness: This is probably one of the biggest goals in ritual. It's the reason why we don't just spend the sabbats watching internet videos about them. We have to participate! Wiccans alter consciousness in ritual because temporarily changing the state of our mind means we're open to the subtle shifting energies of the spiritual worlds. The simply act of casting a circle and setting up your sacred space is an act of consciousness shifting. The change in scenery and action tells your brain, "Hey, something special is about to happen!" Wiccans don't need to use drugs or alcohol in ritual because we can safely alter our consciousness with the many tools rituals bring us.

- Focus/Containment: The best example of this is in the magickal rituals. The ritual circle works as a container to store magickal energy, to keep it from leaking before it's sent out into the world. In rituals where you're doing inner work that just changes you, ritual can help you keep focused on your goal.

- Being Between the Worlds: Astral projection, hedge-riding, dream work, and pathwalking are all spiritual tasks that are aided by ritual. Every time we cast a circle, we are declaring that the space within is also between. There's an old saying by magick workers: "What happens between the worlds happens in all the worlds."

Steps of Ritual

Although it can be a little different depending on the tradition, most full Wiccan rituals have a set of procedures to set up and break down the space. The Wiccan takes steps leading up to the working itself, then reverses each step until landing at what was the beginning (the circle). Here's the basic outline with eight steps:

Step 1: Cleanse yourself and the space. Become properly prepared

Step 2: Cast the circle

Step 3: Call the four guardians and elements

Step 4: Invoke the Goddess and God
Step 5: Perform the main working (spell, journey, meditation, sabbat observance, etc.)
Step 6: Thank the Goddess and God
Step 7: Bid farewell to the guardians and elements
Step 8: Release the circle

The important thing to remember is that every step of ritual is an important spiritual act that will help along your main working and increase your spiritual energy. If you decide to perform a working within a full ritual, make sure that a good amount of time and energy is paid to each step. In ritual, it's all or nothing.

Making Ritual Meaningful

Not every ritual you do will be absolutely stellar, transforming your life for the better. Frankly, some of them will absolutely suck. In fact, a lot of them will. And I'm not just talking about your teenage years either! Adults end up performing, or being in sucky rituals every once in a while too.

Ritual is like anything meaningful we try to do in our lives. Sometimes we're successful with amazing results, and sometimes we fall flat on our face. And of course sometimes we just end up in the middle, getting the results we wanted, but not necessarily in the way we thought they'd come about.

You might feel silly the first few times you do ritual. If you're not used to raising your arms to the directions or throwing rings of light around your room, you'll probably feel a little awkward at first. That's okay! Relax into that tension, take a breath, and remind yourself of your intention.

If you're like me, you might find yourself having an opposite experience. When I first started doing ritual, I felt like I rocked every single one. My confidence came from my excitement, which was a great tool to fuel my effective ritual.

The problem was, eventually the excitement of doing

something new wore away and I was left with just the ritual itself. I had to actually focus on what I was doing, put in the energy, and generally do the work to make the ritual work. Work? Blah. I didn't want work, I wanted the excitement back!

Looking back, I think the gods temporarily took my excitement away for a purpose. They knew that the energy of my rituals was just being fed by adrenaline and the pursuit of fun. Those can be great tools for ritual, but they shouldn't be the only ones at our disposal.

So I did the work. I did ritual even when I wasn't extremely excited about doing it. I took my time and focused on each individual step, each one being as important as the other. Eventually my excitement to be in circle returned! I had done the work to make each step meaningful and important. I learned that effective ritual isn't done only when we're energetic and happy. Ritual is always meant to transform or move us in some way, no matter what our current mood is saying. Be mindful, give it your all, and you'll be sure to have a meaningful ritual.

Challenges of Ritual for Teens

Since I started practicing Wicca at an age where I had absolutely none of my own money and little space of my own to work with, I had to find creative ways to make ritual work for me. Lack of supplies, space, and even time to have them are all excuses teens can easily find to not do ritual. But don't give up! Wiccans are not quitters, we're doers! We take an honest look at the obstacles standing in our way and figure out how to make our goals work. Where there's a witch, there's a way!

Let's take a look at a few of those obstacles, mostly unique to teens, and how we might find ways around them:

- Money: Unless you're old enough to have your own part-time job or have an allowance, it's unlikely that you have regular access to money. This is seen as one of the biggest obstacles to teen Wicca since our religion tends to really love our "stuff." Finding cheap or free materials for ritual is just a matter of putting your wonderful creative mind (a huge advantage you have as a young person) to work. Does a ritual call for large, colored pillar candles placed at every direction to represent the guardian? Pieces of colored construction paper folded and cut into the shape of the elements will work fine. Does it suggest you wear a specific color of hooded robe for the best benefit? Wear a t-shirt of that color or pin a colorful sheet around you like a toga. Again, get creative and don't always "follow the book" if it's not possible. This whole book is interspersed with cheap or free shortcuts in terms of tools and supplies.

- Space: Indoors, you probably only have your room to do ritual in, which may not be very big. The great thing about solitary rituals is that they never require much space. If your room is so small that you can't cast a circle without having the line of energy run over your dresser or bed, that's okay! Run the energy right through it. Ritual altars can be set up on top of dressers or even on your bed if you don't have candles or things that can tip and spill. The most helpful thing to remember with limited ritual space is that if it's small, it should at the least be as clean as possible. Clean spaces allow energy to flow more freely. When I was 16, that was about my only motivation to keep my room clean.

- Privacy: Rituals should not be interrupted if you can help it. I grew up in a big family so I always had a sibling or my mother knocking on my door for some reason or another. The best way I found to get around that is to either wake up really early in the morning (before anyone else gets up) to do ritual, or wait until long after anyone else goes to bed. Of course, that also means you'll have to be quiet and whisper your speaking parts. If your family is particularly accepting of your beliefs, you can just honestly tell them you're doing ritual after dinner and can't be disturbed. Hang a "Ritual in Progress" sign on your door as a reminder.

• Time: Most teenagers have schedules that rival any professional adult businessperson. Between studying, family obligations, and sometimes part-time jobs, the pressure to hold off on doing ritual or to rush through ritual can feel tempting. Wicca is a way of life though, so ritual (and spiritual practice in general) should be worked into your schedule however you can fit it in. It's okay to use time management when planning your rituals. If you want to do a ritual for the full moon but the night of the full moon gives you only 10 minutes of free time, maybe a better night for that is the night before.

Rituals for Two or More

Most aspiring teen Wiccans start out solitary but many come across friends who become interested and want to help out in a ritual, even if they're not quite ready to commit to being fully Wiccan. Group ritual can lead to awesome spiritual and magickal experiences.

Inviting others to join you in ritual can be a great idea as long as everyone involved understands a few things first.

The first thing to consider which might sound a little obvious is that you want everyone involved to understand what will happen on all levels and agree with everything. Everyone should have some idea what to expect, even if it's their first ever ritual. Raising energy affects everyone differently so everyone should know what type of ritual it is and the type of energy required to perform it. Everyone should agree to all aspects of the ritual because agreement means there won't be any surprises to upset the flow of energy. When everyone agrees on a group ritual, a trust is developed that benefits the circle's energy.

You should also think about the type of people entering the circle and how their energy and personality will change and affect the flow of the ritual. You might love your best friend but if he's a big joker who giggles at just about everything, it might not be appropriate for him to join a solemn and serious new-moon ritual. But if it's for a spell to raise joy, he'd be the perfect person to have around. Even if you've learned how to do it by now, remember that not everyone has the ability to shift their energy and mood at the drop of a hat for ritual.

Make sure everyone has a job. It's not fun to be in a ritual where you're just standing there with nothing to do. Boredom distracts from the energy. Ritual should be fun and exciting, even if the goal is a serious one. If the only thing your fellow ritualists do is help direct energy, that's at least something. Ritual is not a spectator sport.

Lastly, and most simply, make sure everyone knows exactly what they're supposed to be doing. Does Johnny know that he's supposed to be calling the guardians and does Cara know that she's casting the circle? Explaining roles in the middle of ritual can interrupt the flow of energy and make it harder to focus and get back on track. This isn't just something for teens to consider either. I've been to too many group rituals where people are dished out important roles right in the middle of ritual. The person with the new role gets flustered, slightly panics with performance anxiety, and the whole thing ends up being sloppy and rushed. Be prepared.

Ritual for Every Day and Life

The thing about ritual is that the more you do it, the more it becomes a part of you, part of your human nature. Eventually, the steps and moves of ritual will feel as natural to you as tying your shoes. But it will also challenge you. It challenges you to look into the depth of your soul and the heights of your spirit. Ritual will allow you to dig deep into your inner shadows and grant you wings to fly back up.

Rituals aren't just opportunities for play-acting that set the stage for magick. They're methods that give us the eyes to see the world anew. All rituals are meant to shape and transform us. Through ritual, Wiccans are forever changing and growing into something greater.

Chapter 5

Magick, Power, and Ethics

Simply put, magick is the art and science of causing change to occur in accordance with your will. Okay, that's not very simple unless we know what each of those things mean. To understand what magick is, we have to break down that definition in each of its parts.

Magick is an Art

There is a lot of beauty in creating magick. When you quiet down or excite your mind and open yourself up to the forces of nature, it's like living poetry in the soul. The Wiccan altar is like the painter's canvass.

Your wand or hands are the brush. The energies you call upon and direct are your paints. Anyone can use a brush and some paint, but it takes practice and deep self-listening to create works of art. The right shades have to be blended together until you learn the right combinations for the visual effect you'd like. The same is true with magick.

We call magick an art because it first arises from the soul. It's the first act that inspires us. In magick, we take inspiration from all over. The trees, wind, and lightning are our muses and when we listen to them, another well of magick opens up for us.

When we look at magick as an art, we realize that it's not exact and even if it were, you wouldn't get good results without putting your heart and soul into it too. I can give you a spell that you could do perfectly, mixing together all the right ingredients and saying all the right things. But if it lacks energy and passion, it will fall flat. That's why spells are much more than recipes you can throw together from a book. Acts of magick require us to work from deep within, and then reach outward to the natural world.

Magick is a Science

That process of reaching outward to the natural world is where the science of magick comes into play. Laurie Cabot, founder of the Cabot Tradition of Witchcraft based in Salem, Massachusetts, was instrumental in putting forth the idea of magick as a science. Her idea that magickal theory derives from scientific ideas is really new though. Aleister Crowley was writing about this long before, but Cabot really sought to fuse the ideas into the witchcraft of America.

Since the time Laurie Cabot began to place a focus on the science of magick, we've learned so much as a society about energy, the mind, the body, and how it all relates to each other. One of the first things we learn in magick is how to still the body and quiet the mind. Even for advanced practitioners, these techniques are still the fundamental essentials of any magickal process. Even if it seems boring at first, learning to master the mind is essential before we can really begin to work effective magick.

We all know that the mind formulates thoughts and puts those thoughts into action in the body. That's the function of the brain. It's just the way our human bodies work. As a science, magick is an extension of the mind's influence, causing change to occur in more than just our own bodies.

The Hermetic Principles

Understanding how magick works on an energetic level is easy once you learn about the Hermetic Principles. The principles are a set of "magickal laws" (just as the law of gravity is a scientific law) that explain how all energy in the universe works. Here's a short explanation of all seven principles.

Mentalism – The Principle of Mentalism states, "The all is mind, the universe is mental." That means that our human minds, the minds of all thinking beings on this planet, and the gods themselves are all one. We each have our own thoughts and feelings, but they are reflections and aspects of this one great mind. This explains how one person's psychic energy affects another person, even without them always meaning for it to. Wiccans and other magick-workers learn to control and focus our thoughts to direct energy in a way that is positive and correct for all involved.

Correspondence – The Principle of Correspondence tells us that all things in the universe have things that relate to another thing. The red rose corresponds to love because it's the color of a healthy beating heart. The dollar or pound signs relate to prosperity and abundance because they're marked on our paper money. The circle corresponds to the sun because that's the shape it forms from our perspective on Earth. Through correspondence, we can affect things that are not near us. I can work a spell to heal my mother who lives four states away by having a photo of her on my altar. Her image in the pictures corresponds to her physical body.

Vibration – "Nothing rests, everything moves" is what the Principle of Vibration tells us. This one is interesting because it's something scientists have only recently confirmed. All matter contains molecules of energy that are constantly moving. Even if the object is moving so slowly that we cannot see the object moving, there is still energy within it buzzing about. Magick requires movement, whether internal or external. When we work magick, we're programming these vibrations to vibrate in a coordinated way, to align with whatever our goal is.

Polarity – The Principle of Polarity states that everything is dual and has a pair of opposites. The Goddess and God would be the most basic example of this in Wicca. Some people get hung up on polarity, thinking that everything has an opposite that is completely different. An example of this would be the Devil of Christianity. Their Devil is seen as the opposite of Christ, evil in every way. In Wicca, there is no absolute evil, other than the incorrect things we as humans bring into the world. The Principle of Polarity tells us that though everything has an opposite, these opposites are more of a system of degrees. So instead of having a perfectly true color of red and one perfectly true color of blue, we realize that all reds are red and all blues are blue, just to varying shades and degrees. Magick works by seeing where something is lacking, and makes up for it by increasing or decreasing that thing's intensity along its poles.

As an example, think of healing magick. Wiccans often heal by sending a person light or life-force energy. This would be the opposite of the most extreme form of illness, which is death. By sending energy that is the supposed "opposite" of death, we pull that person back towards a healthier side of that spectrum.

Rhythm – Everything has a beginning and an ending, a rise and fall, an expansion and a return. This is a powerful truth that Wiccans hold sacred as we see it within everything in nature. As the wheel turns, nature seems to die back and then is reborn in the spring. It has its ups and downs, just as our magick does. Causing change with magick means tapping into the rhythm of our selves and what we're changing. Since magick always follows the path of least resistance, it finds its own rhythm in whatever is happening. Magick-workers might also call this "stepping into the current", which is the result of developing the magickal mind. Stepping into the current helps you stay within the rhythm of nature which will further your magickal goals. This is the result of daily spiritual practice.

Cause and Effect – The Principle of Cause and Effect tells us that everything happens for a reason, even if that reason is unknown to us. The reason might be just or it might not, but there's still always a reason. Magick teaches us personal responsibility. Every time you change something with magick, you change yourself. It's up to you to make the good choices required to help you succeed in life. Wicca has a law of return: whatever you send outside of yourself, will return to you in some form. We will look into that more in a later chapter, but this principle gives us a good preview.

Gender – The gender principle is as simple as it sounds; all things have gender. Don't get too wrapped up in this though. This principle is sometimes distorted to say, "All things are one gender or another" or all female or all male. This is untrue and it is quite the opposite of the gender principle. All things, including humans, have varying degrees of gender. All individuals who identify as men also have female properties, both physical and spiritual, and vice versa.

The Witches' Pyramid

Now that we have a basic understanding of what the Hermetic Principles are, hopefully you have some idea of how magick works. The next system we'll look at – the witches' pyramid – explains why magick works and what the Wiccan or magician has to do to get that magick to be a success.

The pyramid is broken up in four sections, usually seen in this order. Some systems switch the order but it doesn't actually matter. They are:

TO KNOW – TO WILL – TO DARE – TO KEEP SILENT

These are four small statements that seem like they'd be pretty simple, although there's actually a lot going on there. Let's break them down one by one and look at how each one plays out its essential role in our magick.

First, we must know. Above the ancient entryway into the Oracle at Delphi is written the words "know thyself." This is the first essential thing we need for magick to manifest. We have to know our world around us and (most importantly) ourselves. Do you want to know one of the great mystical, hidden, secrets of magick? Of course you do! Well, it's not so much of a secret if you talk to anyone who has been doing magick for a while. The secret is that magick first and foremost changes you before it changes anything else, even if what you're changing looks like its "outside" of you.

On a basic level, to know means that we have to have a good understanding of the situation and our role within it. We have to discover if the thing we believe we want to happen, is something we truly want. Sometimes what we think we want is the exact opposite of what we really want on the soul level. This is where journaling and meditation come in. Self-knowledge can only come with sitting with yourself and paying attention to you. Give all those parts of you a chance to speak.

Will is a funny thing. If I asked you to tell me what will is, one of the first things to come to mind is willpower, that pure grunting force you use to push through difficult tasks. I'm not really sure how that definition came to be, but it's not really true. Will is the core of our entire essence as magickal people. It's that point where desire, power, and the choice to take action all meet.

There are big and small acts of will that we use all the time. You've probably already sensed that learning Wicca and the practice of magick takes a lot of work and study. Reading this book and taking the necessary steps is an act of will. You had the desire to learn and the power to step into that choice and take action. Even if the process of attaining this book and reading it doesn't seem like a big deal to you, it is, in fact, an act of will.

Big acts of will are those things that take a long time to come together. They're what my teacher T. Thorn Coyle describes as "the large arches of our life." What are those big things you want out of life? What is your purpose, your destiny? It's okay if you don't know that right now. It takes a lot of work to get glimpses of our destiny! But being willing to discover that, is a step that even few adults take today.

Small acts of will help build up that larger will. An example of a small act of will is the two-mile walk I take each night to keep my health up. I don't always want to do it. Those times when I don't feel like going for a walk but do it anyway are small acts of will. You might also say that studying well for the SAT exam to get into a good college is a small act of will. They're the driving acts of power that propel us into making decisions that feed the larger will.

Daring is usually thought of as coming after will, but it could be before that also. There's no real order to the statements of the pyramid, as long as all of them are present. I like seeing "to dare" after will because it makes a lot of sense to me. You can be willing to make something happen, but without daring to do it, it's all just in your head. Having the will to go on my walks every night on its own isn't actually enough unless I show up and do it. I know, it sounds like an obvious fact, but you'd be amazed at some of the magick-workers I've met who think they can make things happen by will alone.

When will is followed up by daring, we have the action itself. Let's use meditation as an example because some people can struggle with it. I *know* that meditation makes me feel better, helps me make better decisions, and increases my personal power. With this self-knowledge, I decide that I'm *willing* to make meditation a regular practice in my day. So I set up a time to do it each day. Then I actually sit on my floor and do it every morning, regardless of how sleepy or busy I am. I *dare* to show up and meditate, even when resistance pops up inside me.

Although it appears at the end of the statement of the pyramid, silence can be a part of the magick-worker's entire process. There's a lot of discussion over what silence means in the pyramid. Most take it to mean that before and after working magick, you should not speak of it.

Anderson Feri teacher, Anaar, once asked her teacher Cora, to tell her about silence. Cora Anderson was a simple yet wise woman. She simply said, "Well, keeping the lid on the pot cooks the food faster and it tastes better." The same can be said for our magick. Let it cook for a while. Talking about these things has a tendency to let the steam out of them. That's not to say a spell won't work if you tell a friend about it. But be aware, you might find that it takes longer to come into being and might not have the same kick to it.

Silence helps us grow our power even when we're outside of the circle. It doesn't mean you shouldn't speak, but that you're choosing your words carefully and honestly. A Wiccan is as good as his or her word. Lying, gossiping, and blurting out every random thought that enters our brains (especially on the internet) knots up our personal energy and causes us to be generally less-effective at working magick. I have a big mouth and after practicing Wicca for most of my life, I'm still learning the lessons of silence. When I feel the need to react quickly with my voice (or my fingers if online), I take a breath, walk away, then come back to respond a little later. It's a lesson I'm still doing my best to learn.

Power

All magick runs on power. Power is simply energy that has gathered and accumulated to a degree where something can be done with it. Everyone has energy (or else our bodies and minds couldn't work), but do we all have power? One of the goals of Wiccan spiritual practice is to be a generating source of constant power. We seek empowerment.

Power is too often seen as a dirty word in our culture. We hear phrases like "power corrupts" that makes us think the path to living in greater power means a path of self-servitude, manipulation, or greed. Simply put, that's just garbage! Power, like all energy, is a neutral force. It's what you do with it that counts. There is always a choice.

In many magickal traditions you'll hear the statements *power over* and *power with*. Power over is the use of power for dominance, control, or harm. Power with is the use of power in the spirit of cooperation and self-change. Wiccans prefer power with, not just because of the set of ethical standards many of us live by, but because the use of power with, is just more sustainable. Let's use an example.

Let's say you're part of a sports team that has a really important game coming up. While other team members might be praying for a win, you decide to work some magick to give your team a unique edge.

Using power over, you might enchant the opposite team to perform poorly or make the conditions of the playing field unfavorable to them. Using power with, you would instead enchant your own mind to become focused and clear. You might call upon the elemental energies of the playing field to grant you strength. By using power with, you're effecting change within yourself which will stick around after the game. Had you used the power for dominance and control, you'd know that not only was the game not fair, but you've depleted your energy by sending it out onto someone else for negative means. Again, Wiccans want to live empowered lives, not depleted ones.

Learning Wicca by living its philosophy and practicing its rituals means you'll naturally collect power as you go. Every day we get to choose between standing in power, or standing in a state of depletion. Which will you choose?

The Three Types of Power

Although all power essentially comes from the same place, it's helpful to divide it up into the three types that are most common to Wiccans and other magick-workers. Once we know the types of power, we'll be able to recognize all the places it streams from in ritual and day-to-day life.

Personal Power – This power comes directly from you. It's the power you were born with and naturally gifted by your ancestors and the power you accumulate through regular spiritual practice. Personal power is very precious and some beginner Wiccans make the mistake of using only personal power for every need. Although we can always regenerate our personal power (we do that every time we eat and sleep), doing that can make us feel tired and depleted. Personal power works best when it is in harmony and cooperation with the other two types.

Environmental Power – This is the power of the natural world. Not just the Earth around you, but also the sky above and the planets and stars beyond that. As a nature-based religion, Wiccans work closely with environmental power. It's the easiest type of power to draw from and has a gentle feel to it that mixes well with our personal energy. Technically, our bodies themselves are the byproduct of environmental power. Any time you work with the sun, moon, plants, or animals, you're working with environmental power.

Divine Power – The third type of power comes from the gods themselves. This is the power of the Goddess, God, and the spirit-force that moves between them. We call upon divine power any time we ask the Goddess and God to be with us in circle for a ritual, to when we ask them to guide our day in morning devotionals.

Divine power is a little more complicated because both personal and environmental power are also manifestations of the divine, just in more concentrated forms. That said, once you're able to sense energy well, you'll notice that divine power just *feels* a little different than personal and environmental.

The reason why I like to explain the different types of power is that once you realize there are other sources to pull energy from besides yourself, you'll have more power available to fuel your magickal work. Let's use a practical example.

Wiccans use all kinds of different methods to cast a circle and the big difference is usually the type of energy they use. Some Wiccans are very adamant about using personal power, which is then returned to the athame at the end of the working. Others say it is far better to use environmental power so that your personal power remains strong for the magick itself. I actually like to use both methods depending on what I'm doing. A protective ritual would mean I'd cast a circle with personal power (I'm "staking my territory" in this way) and a healing ritual would mean I'd use environmental power (the Earth is humanity's prime source of healing).

Exercise – Directing Environmental Power

We've already gone over how to direct personal power since that's the default most Wiccans use to conjure up power. Once you know how to call energy from the environment around you, you have a choice in where the power comes from and how much of it you use. Everyone loves more choices!

When directing environmental power, it would obviously be ideal to be outside in some natural setting. It's easier to make a connection with the elements when you're physically surrounded by their pure states. This can still be done indoors since the elements exist everywhere, but you'll find that working directly in nature (even if it's just out on your back porch) just feels better.

Get in a comfortable state and slow your breathing down. If there's a rhythmic wind blowing about, try matching the pace of your breath to that. Sense the power of the environment all around you. Feel yourself connected to the pulse of nature and all life within it.

Open up your hands, palms facing outside of you. Begin to feel all of the natural environment around you buzzing with power. You may even visualize it as a gentle green glow hovering above the leaves of the trees and alongside every blade of grass.

With your imagination, draw that energy down from all these sources and see it collect between the palms of your hand. With the energy now in your grasp, you can do whatever you normally would with it like cast a circle or charge up an object. With the circle casting, you would draw the energy into the line of the circle on the ground rather than have it collect in your hands.

Once you're done using the elemental power, it's considered polite to send any excess energy you don't use back into the ground for the nourishment of the planet.

Exercise – Directing Divine Power

For most rituals, divine power is generally called at the start of the rite during the invocation and that sets up the flow of divine power for the rest of the working. However, you can intentionally call upon divine power just like with environmental power. Usually this is easier to do once your own connection to your gods has become established and comfortable.

To call divine power, you start just like you do with the previous method; stilling the body and slowing down the breath. This time, turn your palms up to the sky and say a prayer to the divine, asking the God, Goddess, or both, to lend you energy.

Feel it streaming down from above you, usually seen as pure white light. The gods aren't actually "above" in the sense that they live in some kind of heavenly world. They're above, below, and all around. But for the purpose of this working, I find it helpful to draw that divine energy down from the sky above. The sky is vast and limitless, just like the reach of the gods themselves.

Divine power is a wonderful energy to call when you want to bless yourself, your room, or if you just want to feel the presence of the Goddess and God around you. Calling divine power can make you feel happy and even give you a little rush of energy, while environmental power helps you stay grounded and anchored.

Being a Strong Container

If power is a collection or force of energy, then we can think of the body, mind, and soul as a container for that energy. The body itself is like the cup, the sacred tool of the element of water. We're constantly filling it up and emptying it back out, both physically and energetically. Choosing to stand in the flow of greater personal power means keeping our "cup" full and nourished.

As you grow in your personal practice and begin to feel comfortable with a lot of the workings, you'll find that your energy levels increase, your outlook on certain situations might change, and you're thought processes will become deeper and a bit more thoughtful.

With all of this new power coming in, our bodies as containers will begin to expand a little to take in more. It's exactly like exercising a muscle; the work you do to put that muscle into motion means it will expand and grow bigger.

Usually feeling yourself expand is an awesome feeling and it shows up differently in everyone. For me, it was the deep hunger for learning. I used to go to the library and spend entire weekends devouring book after book. It didn't even matter that I wasn't actually absorbing very much of it because for me, it was all about the pleasure of doing it.

Sometimes having your container expand is a little uncomfortable, just like the sore muscles that come right after working out. In developing a spiritual and magickal practice like Wicca and working with these energies, you might have days where you feel really tired, like you just can't hold onto very much energy. Or you might feel irritable and cranky. This is a very normal adjustment process to working with new energy, as any athlete in training will tell you.

When Magick Fails

Sometimes spells don't work or you feel like you just didn't get much out of a ritual. I'll let you in on a little secret right now – it happens to all of us! Even the most experienced Wiccans who have been practicing for their entire life find that their magick occasionally fumbles. Sometimes it's because of things that are outside of our control, and sometimes it's from steps that we missed or factors we didn't take into account.

Here's a list of common reasons why magick will fail. You can easily see for yourself which are caused by us as practitioners and which are circumstantial.

- No Physical Follow-Up – I put this first because it seems to be the most common. Magick, meant to affect the physical world requires physical follow-up. If you do a spell to get a job but don't put in applications, it's going to fail. It sounds obvious but you'd be amazed how some people (adults included) think they can get whatever they want without doing any worldly actions.

- Mental State – Maybe you were having a bad day and couldn't shake it before you stepped into circle. Eventually you'll figure out how to shift your energy so it's stable for ritual, but it takes practice and we all struggle with it on occasion.

- Physical State – Magick is less likely to be successful if you're sick or tired.

- Timing – The planets, moon, and sun all affect the energy here on Earth. Sometimes the astrological conditions in the sky were just totally unfavorable and mucked up the working.

- Lack of Focus – Magick should be precise if you expect it to change anything. Was your goal specific, clear, and attainable?

- Lack of Effort – It takes effort to raise the energy needed for magick to work. While we'd love to be able to say a rhyme and swing a wand around for instant magick, it just doesn't work that way. Put some muscle into your magick.

- Divine Intervention (Grace) – This is a little less common, but sometimes when the gods know that something we're doing will end up very badly for ourselves or someone else, they will jump in and stop it. The gods are more likely to do this with beginner magick-workers because they understand that you're learning. But don't expect them to always stop a misfired spell! More often than not, they'll want us to learn from it so we know what to change for the future.

You might have noticed that "missing an ingredient" or "saying a word wrong" are not on that list. Movie depictions of magick sometimes make it seem like spellwork is simple chemistry that doesn't involve physical effort beyond getting each step right. Magick is a science yes, but it's not an exact science.

When Magick Succeeds

Ok, so you've done a spell or other magickal working and it worked! Now what? First, pat yourself on the back for a job well done, then make sure you think about doing the following.

- Record your results in your magickal journal or book of shadows. Write about what you did, the working you used, how you felt physically and mentally before you did it, and even what phase the moon was in if you know it. All of these things can give you hints about how to set yourself up for successful magick next time.
- If the spell is still in the process of manifesting, continue to do work in the physical world to follow up.
- Show some gratitude. If you called upon a specific deity, element, etc., take a few moments during your daily practice to give heartfelt thanks.

General Ethics in Magick

You didn't think you could just go about zapping away at friends and enemies alike, did you? Good! Because if you're going to be Wiccan you have you follow some basic guidelines that go along with it.

The primary guideline where magick is concerned is the Wiccan Rede: *"Do as ye will, an it harm none."*

Now, there's a lot of debate about exactly what that means. A lot of Wiccans interpret the rede to mean that you should absolutely never cause harm, regardless of the reason. In reality though, every time we walk down the street we're destroying life forms with our feet, so it's really sort of impossible to never cause any harm. Instead, many Wiccans believe it means that we should avoid causing harm to the best of our ability. You can think of it essentially as a form of the Golden Rule: "Do unto others as you would have them do unto you."

Why do we have this rede and what good is it? Simply put, Wicca strives to create an environment that's harmonious for the practitioner. We know that it's silly to cause intentional harm because we'd just be putting more destruction into the world when what we really need is healing.

If harm is coming our way, we first take measures to protect ourselves from that harm. And if it reaches us, we will neutralize it and ground it down into the Earth to be transformed into something helpful. We don't bother sending it back because that would just put us in a constant bounce-back battle with that energy. It's better to just take hold of it when it comes to us and end it right there. But what if someone is intentionally causing us harm and they won't stop? That leads us to our next topic...

Binding, Banishing, and Cursing

Binding is a popular method of stopping harm in its tracks and the person causing the harm. It's a harmless way to stop a harmful person without hurting them or taking away their free will. The point of a binding is to create a conditional barrier around the person that keeps them from committing acts of harm. That's it.

I'll admit, I did a lot of binding when I was in middle school and high school. Bullies just loved to target me out and it wasn't often easy to avoid them. The tricky part about bindings is that they're only temporary. You usually have to keep the physical materials of the spell safely intact or it will become unraveled.

Even then, bindings tend to lessen in strength as time goes on. Whenever I would bind a bully in school it would usually only last for a couple of months. Then again, the type of binding you do can influence that timeframe too. I'll share a binding spell you can do in the spells section of this book.

Binding is an ethical topic because some people believe it's not right to bind someone because you're affecting their free will by keeping them from doing something they want to do, harming you. I disagree. If we look at the Wiccan Rede, it's clear to see that we ourselves are included in the "harm none" portion of it. Allowing someone to continuously harm us without taking any action is a violation of the rede. Go with your own personal instincts and form your own opinion on whether or not it's right to bind someone. And of course you should always ask yourself this question: "Have I done everything I can in the physical world to stop this first?"

Banishing is a broad term and actually doing it is very different depending on what you're banishing and the intent of that banishing. Wiccans frequently banish negative energy in general. It's the theme of the work we do on the waning moon. When the moon decreases in power, we diminish things in our life that aren't helpful to our goals. There are three major types of banishment that most Wiccans practice.

The most common and easy kind of banishment is on yourself. In Wicca we're always trying to get in touch with our inner being so we have to do a lot of work to get rid of all the crud that stops us from getting there. This is when we banish things like bad habits, unhealthy egos, resentment, poor self-image, etc. This is the work of a lifetime, and not something that's just done once. Our culture piles on so much stress, negativity, and pressure (especially for teens!) that banishment of unhelpful things within the self needs to be a part of our spiritual practice constantly.

The next type of banishment is on your personal space. Cleansing of the home and other places around you is a great way to make sure that none of that muck sticks to you and latches onto your own personal energy. One of the most popular ways to banish negativity from a space is to burn white sage. The smoke of the sage is purifying and clears away all dense and harmful vibrations. If you live with parents who don't like you burning things, this might be impossible to do. Instead, you might close your eyes and imagine bright white fire descending from the sky and sweeping through your personal space. That's just as effective as burning sage in my opinion (and it smells nicer).

Finally, we get to the type of banishment that's debated by some Wiccans and is the reason why it's in the "ethics" section; the banishment of people. Banishing someone is a more extreme kind of binding. You're not just stopping someone in your life from causing more harm, you're asking that they be completely removed from your life entirely. Usually this means the person will be forced to avoid you entirely, should they come anywhere near you. The magick would pull them away into the opposite direction. Sometimes if the banishment is strong enough it means the person will just move away to another location.

The first major banishment I did was on a school bully who was so focused on making my life miserable that I feared for my safety almost every day. My school knew about it but very little was done. When physical abuse would happen, it would always end with the promise that more would be coming. Not knowing what else to do, I turned to a banishment. I performed the banishment on a dark moon day and the following month, he had moved out of the state with his parents and I never saw him again.

You really have to decide for yourself whether or not a banishment is worth it. It really isn't right to just send packing any person who annoys you. If someone is causing me trouble I generally follow a simple timeline of actions based on the danger I'm facing. If one thing doesn't work, I move on to the next one:

Physical worldly action – Protection – Binding – Banishing

The last topic involving receiving, or causing harm, is cursing. It's a widely acceptable fact that cursing has no place within Wicca. What exactly do we mean by cursing? Generally, a curse involves actively projecting harm towards a target. The goal is not just keep them from harming (binding) or to get them to go away (banishing) but rather to make them suffer in some way. There are a few reasons Wiccans don't curse:

- Cursing is against the rede because they do more than eliminate harm, they cause it proactively. Wiccans believe that it's not up for us to determine the suffering of another. Curses cause one to take on the role of "judge, jury and executioner."
- They're very hard to do. Curses take an enormous amount of life-force energy to call up and maintain. And even if you get that far, you still have the other person's natural energy barriers to work through. Neutralizing the harm they send your way is just easier.
- Curses can backfire easily, and often do (see the section below on the Threefold Law).

The Law of Threefold Return

The law of three isn't really an ethical rule as much as it is a statement of cause and effect. Simply put, the Wiccan law of threefold return is that whatever magick you work that gets sent outside of yourself (for good or bad) will come back to you times three. It will come back either once with three times the amount of force as the original working or it will come back three times with the same force that you sent it out with.

A basic example of the law of three working in a helpful way is healing magick. If I send healing energy to a friend and it helps him get better, the law of three states that I'll get three times that energy back. It could either come back to me when I need it (like when I'm sick myself) or it'll come back right away and give my immune system a nice little boost.

On the other hand, the threefold law applies to all things, not just positive workings. So if I were to throw a curse at someone I dislike that causes them to trip and fall, I might find myself falling down a flight of stairs, sustaining three times the injuries that my opponent received. Using this example, it's easy to see why Wiccans would avoid cursing, even if one were okay with causing harm. After all, why bother doing something that's just going to cause more trouble for yourself?

We might say that this is a form of karma. Although, traditionally, karma is thought to have an equal impact on someone from what they sent out, not threefold. So why does magick return times three rather than times one? The theory is that since you're calling upon power that effects a change in your energy, the energy around you, and the energy of the person or object, you're really casting a spell upon three "worlds". Still with me so far? No? Okay, let's use another example. If you throw a rock from outside a pond into a pond, it creates ripples. The rock doesn't just fall into place at the bottom of the pond without doing anything else. And it doesn't just cause one ripple, it causes a bunch of them, not including the waves it makes as it sinks down into the bottom. Our magick always affects more than what's on the surface, even if we only mean for it to change something simple.

The law of three is sometimes debated by Wiccans who feel it doesn't make sense that everything we do should return to us with so much greater force than we sent it out with. Whether you believe the law of three works or not, I suggest using it, like the rede, as a guide map along your way.

As we grow, our sense of ethics and personal morals will change and evolve. When in doubt, use the rede as a guide first then check in with the gods. Ask them for help and advice about how you should move forward. If you're still, and listen closely, they will speak to you and let you know.

Chapter 6

Topics for the Teen Wiccan

Now that you have a decent grounding in the core practices and beliefs of Wicca, we can start to talk about how your new path will affect other areas of your life. It can be tricky for anyone to start out on a new path. It being likely that you're not quite out on your own yet, you probably have certain limitations that you'll have to find creative ways to work around. A lot of this will center around looking for reliable teachings. Some of it will involve dealing with touchy situations like unsupportive family or harassment in school.

A lot of what we'll go over here will be based on my personal experiences. Since I started practicing Wicca right at the "teen threshold" of life (twelve years old), I got to experience a full spectrum of things that studying Wicca at a young age will bring. That said, everyone's situations and experiences will be different than my own and so my advice won't always apply. As always, trust your intuition and seek out the advice of a mentor you trust whenever you can.

Finding a Teacher vs. Self-Training

Since Wicca began, it's long been a tradition of students and teachers. Back in the '50s when Wicca was first starting to grab a foothold, information about magick, witchcraft, and nature-based spiritual studies was really difficult to come by on your own. People would have to search long and hard just to find a copy of Gardner's early books like *High Magic's Aid*. Even then you'd have to read between the lines because the information presented was cloaked in mystery.

Because of how difficult it was to find information on one's own, the tradition of finding a teacher or a teaching coven to train with was born. Seekers to the Craft would usually train with a teacher for at least a year and a day before receiving full initiation. Before that, a student might have a self-dedication rite to declare their intention before the gods. Essentially, if you wanted to learn Wicca but couldn't find a physical teacher, you'd be out of luck.

Lucky for us, the combination of an explosion of interest in Pagan practices coupled with the start of the information age changed all of that. By the time the early '80s rolled around, people interested in learning Wicca could find easily find resources to do so.

However easy it is for us to find resources on Wicca today, no one can underestimate the value of a real teacher. We'll go over how to find a teacher in a bit. But for now, let's go over the perks of having a teacher, should you have access to one. There are obviously many benefits to having a physical teacher:

- Finding a reliable teacher means having access to reliable information. Book sources for information can sometimes be tricky to validate and even more so for internet sources.
- The teacher will have personal stories and experiences to share that make it easier to learn. Books can do this (I try to share some stories of my own in this one), but stories that come up in spontaneous conversation tend to stick better.
- Teachers can help you troubleshoot. In other words, if you're having trouble with a magickal technique or understanding a spiritual ideal, a teacher can get into the nooks and crannies of whatever is holding you back.
- A teacher in Wicca often relates to a mentor in life. Mentors, especially at a young age, can be really helpful in guiding you through these sometimes-chaotic years. Everyone can always use someone to talk to, young and old alike. I'm in my mid-twenties as I write this and I still have mentors I talk to from my teenage years. A couple of them

were Wiccan teachers I knew at a young age.

- A lot of people just learn better through speech rather than reading. If you're what's called an "auditory learner", having a teacher is especially helpful.
- Depending on the teacher, you might have someone willing to guide you through the steps of ritual and magickal workings. A physical teacher will be able to spot the changes in energy that come up and make suggestions on how you might gain more from the ritual next time.

Let's say you either can't find a teacher or you just prefer to study on your own. There's no shame in that. Many of the most talented Wiccans I know were self-trained at an early age and turned out to be incredible thinkers and teachers themselves. Studying on your own requires a lot of personal discipline, self-awareness, and patience. Let's go over a few of the big benefits to training on your own:

- You get a self-paced training program. This is especially good news if you like to take your time and slowly incorporate what you study into your personal practice. A physical teacher will require you to study on your own anyway, but learning by yourself means you get to control your own pace.
- If you're under 18 and your guardians don't give permission for you to meet with a physical teacher, that option might be out even if you do have access to one. Personal study takes away some of the stress of having a guardian becoming comfortable with a teacher. And Wiccan teachers will usually not teach minors without the permission of a legal guardian anyway.
- Freedom of experience. There are many wonderful Wiccan teachers out there but sometimes even the wisest of them can get caught up in recreating their own experiences. A

good teacher should give personal anecdotes along the way but some fall into the "you have to do it this way" trap. With self-study, you don't have someone trying to squeeze your personal experiences into whatever their tight little box is. You have the freedom to inform yourself based on your own experiences.

- If your interests are more eclectic (meaning you like a variety of practices from different traditions), you'll have more opportunities to dip into areas of study that interest you. There's no pressure to study one entire system through to completion. That said, there is a lot of value in sticking with a stable system of study. But if you're not ready for that, then self-study is the way to go.

Now that you know some of the pros and cons of learning from a teacher versus learning on your own, you should be in a good place to really think about which direction you would like to go. Of course, you might not have a choice. Many teens don't have access to physical teachers and so self-study would be the only option for now. You can always find a mentor in later years.

Finding a Teacher

Let's say you decide that having a teacher is the right way to go for you. Where do you start? There's an old saying that goes, "When the student is ready, the teacher will appear." I partly agree with that since I think the gods help guide us to the knowledge we need at the time, but I'm not totally satisfied with it either. Finding a teacher (especially one that's just right for you) can be difficult and time-consuming work.

The first thing you have to think about is your parents or guardians. Legally in the United States, parents have the right to decide how their kids are educated. If you've already spoken with your parents about having a physical Wiccan teacher and they object, that pretty much stops the search right there.

On the other hand, if your parents are open to the idea, you should involve them in the process as much as possible, even as far as having them help reach out to teachers for you. My first adult teacher was a lovely woman named Tina, the mother of a new friend I had made in middle school. I was actually really enjoying my self-study up until that point, but once I found out I had the chance at having a teacher, I jumped on it. After warming my mother up to the idea, she and Tina met in a coffee shop to chat about what I'd be learning, what I'd be doing, etc. That one meeting eased any concern my mother had and I was good to go.

My first adult teacher as well as my first peer teacher before her, were brought to me almost by coincidence. But if you already have the parental green light, there's no reason why you can't do some active searching. Here are a few search methods to get you started:

- Online resources like The Witches Voice (WitchVox) in the US or The Pagan Federation in the UK are great places to start making contacts. WitchVox for example has profiles of teachers that even indicate whether or not they're accepting students currently. You can also get in touch with well-known Wiccan organizations like Circle Sanctuary or Aquarian Tabernacle Church who are known for connecting people with resources like teachers.
- Social Networking: Although this is an online resource, it deserves a note on its own. Making connections through "someone who knows someone who knows someone" can be an excellent place to start. Once you "friend" a couple of Wiccans or Pagans in your area, you're likely going to find access to many more of them.
- See if there is a local Pagan shop in your area. They will often have classes already set up that you can just walk right on in to! If they don't, you can always go in and try

talking to the staff about connecting you with local resources. Shop owners are usually very well connected and should have some good information for you. Usually if they don't have an answer, they'll be happy to help you find one.

- Using your online search resources, try attending a local Pagan event like a festival or a meetup. This is one of the most popular "old school" methods for connecting with others of like mind.

- If you don't have a Pagan shop in your area and there are no events that you can find, try getting involved with a local Unitarian Universalist church if your town has one. Unitarian Universalism is a faith that widely accepts and embraces other religious practices very openly, especially nature-based faiths like Wicca. Many UU churches have Pagan sub-groups called CUUPS, the Covenant of UU Pagans.

I should also mention that it's pretty easy to receive online distance training in Wicca and certain other traditions of witch-craft these days. However, most online teachers and schools will not accept minors. If they say they don't but you happen to have the support of your guardians behind you, ask them to write an email to the teacher or school asking for an exception. I'd be willing to bet that if a parent or guardian made the initial contact, they'd be more willing to bend the rules for you. Teachers who do distance training and online schools that specialize in Wicca are many. Search around and shop like you would for a prospective college.

Finding Trustworthy Web Resources

Whether you're self-trained or have a teacher guiding you, you'll definitely be using the internet a lot for learning, researching specific topics in your studies, and connecting with other

Wiccans. I started practicing Wicca right around the time when web resources for Pagan studies were just beginning to increase and become reliable. What a huge difference! Books will always have a very strong resource for any budding Wiccan scholar, but having access to essentially any information you could possibly need at your fingertips is groundbreaking. As I write this, I can point out that no other generation beyond mine and yours have had access to information like this. We're very lucky.

But as the comics say, "With great power comes great responsibility." As we all know, the internet comes with its own set of risks and troubles, both in relation to your Wiccan studies and other areas of your life. The most obvious concern for young folk are child predators. Though I will trust that you already know how to avoid those people, so I won't spend more time on it than a quick mention. Needless to say, be smart and remember that people are often not as their online profiles make them seem.

With so many people blogging, micro-blogging, and hosting their own websites, there are about fifty different opinions on any one topic. This is where things get tricky. There's an old joke that goes, "Ask ten Wiccans to define Wicca and you'll get one-hundred answers." Honestly, that's quite true! So the first thing to be aware of is that as soon as you go from reading books to reading websites, you'll be exposed to more perspectives on the Craft than you ever thought possible. In a lot of ways this is wonderful. It's great to get different perspectives and I really encourage you to seek them out. On the other hand, it also means that anyone who reads a magazine article about Wicca can go and design a website for it. The information you get might not be that reliable.

If you find yourself reading web material about Wicca and wonder if it's reliable or not, you can ask yourself a few of these questions:

- What is the mood of the site and the author of the

material? Does the author seem overly opinionated, basing their ideas simply on feelings alone? Material is more likely to be trustworthy if it's a healthy mixture of facts and personal *experiences* rather than just opinion.

- Is the author using too many blanket statements? A blanket statement is something said that's meant to loop many people or ideas into one idea. Although Wicca is a very unique and specific religion, it is also a religion of personal individuals. Even if ten Wiccans are doing the same thing, the reasons they do it and the way they experience it might be totally different. An example of an unreliable blanket statement might be, "All Wiccans pour milk on the ground in honor of Brigid at Imbolc." Certainly some do, but not all of us will. Knowing that there are many ways to do the same thing is important. Be especially cautious of blanket statements that start with, "All Wiccans do this…"
- Does the web material seen overly fantastical, promising riches and beauty based on their "easy three-step spell"? Watch out for online spell-sellers, which pretend to be reliable Wiccan and Pagan sites but are really designed to sell you magickal formula promising amazing super-natural results. Let me break it to you here; spells don't always manifest in mesmerizing and exciting ways. In fact, they usually don't.

With all of those cautionary notes out of the way, I should say that you don't have to be a total paranoid skeptic to enjoy online research on Wicca. As the religion matures and more scholars and elders get their writings on the web, resources become more and more trustworthy. If you go about it in a smart way, you can get a lot of great information online. And the best part is – it's usually free!

Talking to Parents and Family

I almost gave this topic a chapter all on its own, as this is often one of the most difficult situations that teen Wiccans come up against when beginning to explore the religion. When I was a teen, I thankfully had a patient family who were willing to sit down with me and talk about my interests. My mother even took the time to meet with a Wiccan high priestess to talk about what she should expect out of me as I got more involved with it. Sadly, though, I also had many friends who had to stop their studies altogether because their parents and family went absolutely nuts when they found out that their kids were essentially becoming witches.

Obviously everyone's experience is going to be different depending on what your family is like. The process of "coming out" and telling your family about what you believe in is a bit like coming out as lesbian, gay, bisexual, or transgender when you're young. Some families that have conservative Christian values are more likely to be opposed to it than families that are progressive and have more liberal religious philosophies (or no religious connections at all.) I fall under the category of someone who has a progressive family that doesn't really care about religion very much, although most of them would say they're Christian in some way.

That said, you may be very surprised at how your family reacts. You might think that they'll go bonkers when they might just be curious to know more and show an interest in hearing about your newfound philosophies and beliefs. I've known young Wiccans who think that their parents will absolutely hate the thought of Wicca but come to find out that their family either doesn't care at all, or even that they're pretty encouraging. Either way, there are things we can do to prepare for both scenarios.

First things first: I highly recommend that you not drop the "Mom, I'm a witch" bomb. Randomly making a huge statement out of the blue like that during Sunday breakfast is probably the most risky path you could take. Parents and family are more likely to make kneejerk reactions because they weren't expecting it to come up and you haven't given them much time to think about how they feel about it. My experience with knowing a lot of teens who have come out, shows that those situations don't usually turn out so well initially. Instead, you can drop subtle hints that you're interested in things like the spiritual side of nature, meditation, folklore, mythology, and (once you start getting brave) real magick. If you can find a good streaming documentary about modern-day Paganism, suggest it as a family movie based on your historical interest in it. Use how they react to those interests as a gauge to help you determine if it's the right time to come out of the broom closet or not.

When the time comes to have the actual conversation about your personal religious beliefs, prepare yourself with a set of talking points that will help you clearly communicate what you want them to know about. Remember, many people (and probably your parents) will automatically associate anything relating to magick and witchcraft with Satanism, possession, and other icky things that go bump in the night. Because your family will probably be coming from a place that's informed by their past misconceptions, you might have to spend some time talking about what Wicca is not before you can start talking about what Wicca is.

If you're lucky then you might end up in a really supportive family situation where you can practice however you like without interruption. But what if your family goes nuts and forbids it? Here's where a lot of Wiccan authors will tell you, "That's sad, but you'll have to wait until you're older and move out." I am not one of them!

The reality is, you might not have the ability to have a fully set altar with all the bells and whistles out in your room at all times. You might not be able to go out into your back yard and call down the gods surrounded by glowing candles. But the thing is, if you can't do that stuff out in the open, it still doesn't mean you can't practice Wicca. No one can stop you from looking up at the moon and whispering a prayer to the Goddess. No one can stop you from sitting in your bed in the morning to meditate before you start your day. No one can stop you from practicing energy direction or setting positive intentions. The truth is that in many countries teens don't have a whole lot of rights until they turn 18. Your guardians do "own" you to some extent. Just remember, no one can own your heart and what you do with your mind.

Even if you can't have an altar full of fancy tools, you can still have a few tools for your practice that no one will take a second glance at. You can bring these things together for rituals and then keep them in different places when you're done.

- Altar Pentacle – Find a flat stone slab like the ones you can find along creek beds and lake shores. Draw the pentacle on it with chalk and voila! Instant altar pentacle. You can even cut out a sheet of paper into a circle and draw the pentacle on that with a marker. When you're done, shred it up completely and toss it in the trash with other garbage.
- Incense – It's really hard to cover up burning incense, so what could you use on the altar to represent air in its place? Feathers, fallen leaves, or a photo of the sky are great substitutes. I don't like burning incense every day anyway so I keep a small crow feather on my altar instead.
- Candles – It might feel really frustrating to practice Wicca and magick without being able to use candles. There's just something about them that makes the atmosphere feel witchy and ready for action. If you can't use real candles, look for those LED battery-powered candles that many dollar-bargain stores sell. Instead of inscribing your intentions on it, write it on a piece of paper and stick it underneath.
- Chalice – This is an easy one. A chalice is any cup that can

hold water so any cup will do. If you can borrow a wine glass from the kitchen to hold the water it'll feel a bit more "special", but it's not totally necessary.

- Wand – Although a lot of people like to decorate wands with beautiful designs and gemstones, a basic wand is just a stick. There really doesn't need to be more to it than that. If you obtain a wand and need to keep it concealed, leave it in its most natural stickly form. If discovered, no one will be able to tell what it's for.

- Athame – Keeping an athame can be a little trickier than the other tools, but it's still possible to have one. Although they are generally double-sided, you can always borrow a butter knife from the kitchen. That said, the athame should really only be used for directing energy and shouldn't be used to cut things physically. If you use the butter knife, cleanse it well and then keep it somewhere safe so that it's only used for that purpose. The reason I suggest using a butter knife and not a steak knife is that if discovered, the butter knife probably won't make your parents nervous like a sharp one will.

- Divination Tools – Can't keep a crystal ball, deck of tarot cards, or a set of runes? No problem! For basic divination that requires simple yes/no answers, obtain a light-colored stone and a dark-colored stone. The lighter stone is a "yes" while the darker stone is a "no." Pick a stone out of a bag three times and go with what the majority of the three selections were. You can also make a pendulum by tying a stone, acorn, or other object to the bottom of a piece of thread.

- Altar – Any surface can be an altar. A nightstand, dresser, or overturned box are all examples of makeshift altars I've used.

Again, most authors on Wiccan and Pagan topics for teens will tell you to not to practice until you're older if your parents have an issue with it. Personally, I believe that if you think the risk is worth it, you should practice however you like as long as you're not harming yourself or others. In many cases, once family sees that what you're doing is actually helping you to become a better person, they'll come around. And if they don't? Well, that's just more reason to get good grades so you can get an awesome job and move out.

Being Wiccan in Grade School

Here's another topic that could fill an entire chapter on its own. The truth is, the majority of your waking life revolves around school in one way or another. Besides actually attending classes, you also have to think about homework, extracurricular activities, and your social life which is school-based too. If you feel like school is your entire life, you're absolutely right because in a lot of ways, it is!

With school being such a huge part of teen life, the teen Wiccan has to be aware of how practicing Wicca will come up in school-related situations. There are a lot of great benefits to being Wiccan in grade schools, but there are also some concerns you should know about too. Let's go over a few from both sides of that coin.

The first concern is bullying and harassment. Unfortunately, as I write this it seems like bullying is getting worse and worse in the schools in my country. It seems like every day I hear about teens who are going through terrible times because of bullying and other peer-based abuse. While some people might tell you that bullying is "just a part of growing up," let me make something perfectly clear: no one ever has an excuse to abuse you and it should definitely not be something you should get used to or let slide. If you or a friend are the victims of harassment, you need to tell someone because that's just not okay.

Practicing a nature-based faith means that you can now consider yourself a minority. And just like other minority students, you'll be a little more prone to bullying than those who are more "mainstream." I experienced horrific amounts of bullying from the fifth grade all the way up through tenth grade, about five years. Most of that was based on religion since everyone knew I was "that Wiccan guy." Granted, I was blessed to have a few good friends who really helped me through some tough situations, so I was a little more fortunate than some. There were times when I thought that getting through school with my sanity intact would be virtually impossible. But because of my faith in what I was doing and how it helped me, I did.

My point is that even though I'd like to tell you that everyone will treat you exactly the same as before they found out about your interests in Wicca, they probably won't. The truth is, you'll lose some friends and make some enemies. But you might also gain some really great friends in the process. The important thing to know is that through Wicca, you can find your own worth that isn't measured by what other people think of you. If you're doing something that empowers you and connects you to universe, then the people who poke fun and cause trouble for you are less important than you think.

As much as I wish it didn't happen, teachers can sometimes be bullies too. I grew up in a conservative southern town in North Carolina so I had a few negative experiences with teachers based on my faith.

Luckily, most of them worked out well for me in the end. The first problem was in the first year I started practicing Wicca which was when I was in the 7th grade. My science teacher (a very conservative Christian man) went through my bag, took out my copy of *Teen Witch* by Silver Ravenwolf, and confiscated it. He "replaced it" with a pamphlet of verses from the Bible. I marched right down to the administration office and complained to the school counselor who not only got my book back, but forced the teacher to apologize to me.

Sometimes teachers will defend you though. A couple of years after the book incident I found myself with a substitute math teacher while in the 9th grade who told me to take off the pentacle pendant I wore every day. Being a little more bold, I told her no and that it was illegal to ask that of me while other students wore crucifixes. The substitute teacher walked next door to complain to my history teacher that I was causing problems in her classroom. My history teacher spent the next ten minutes telling her that not only could she not ask me to take my pendant off, but that I was a good student and that she should leave my religious views out of the classroom.

Luckily, most of my experiences with teachers were learning experiences. Teachers are in an education industry, so for the most part they'll at least be curious to know a little more about what Wicca is if they don't already know. This is especially true in the higher grades where teachers are more likely to take you seriously and engage in personal conversation with you. In my later years in high school, I had many casual conversations with teachers about my religious philosophy when asked.

Ultimately, the way you handle being Wiccan in school is up to you. All of the stories I just mentioned all came from me being completely open about my faith the whole time I was in school. It was very important for me personally to express my individuality and to show that I was comfortable with myself. However, you might not think that the possible stress is worth it and just keep your practices secret at school. Again, that decision is yours and one that you should spend a good while thinking about.

Generally, even if you are "out" about being Wiccan in school, it's still probably best to keep talk of it to a minimum unless there's a good reason to bring it up. There's power in silence when it comes to magick after all.

Your Changing Mind

One of the major reasons why school can be such a tricky minefield to navigate through is puberty. Growing up and facing the many changes your body and mind go through means that emotions will run high. And where emotion runs high, so does energy. This makes practicing a magick-affirming religion like Wicca very interesting for young people and there are a few things you should be aware of because of that.

Adolescence actually brings you a huge advantage energetically. Because teens have such powerful, emergent energy, you'll find that you can make things happen a lot faster than many other magick-workers. When I was a teen I got used to casting a spell and having it manifest as soon as the next day in many cases. As I got older and entered my twenties, I found that I had to put more energy, focus, and intensity into my magickal projects to get them to manifest quickly. Being a teen is an energetic ace up your sleeve.

The high intensity of energy is the same reason why paranormal phenomena tends to follow teens around a lot. Most poltergeist activity can be chalked up to a child or teen living in the home who's going through a hard time. It's like their energy is just bouncing all over the place with no good channel to move through. The great thing about Wicca is that it can give your energy a good container. Having a strong container for your energy means that you'll have more of it (because less of it is "leaked") and that can help to prevent you from having magickal oopsie moments.

Magickal oopsie moments are also known as "accidental magick." These are like little spells that you send out without realizing it. Usually it happens when your emotions are pitched and you're really focused on what you're feeling. Practicing magick regularly means that you train your body to manifest energy for any sort of purpose. Magickal oopsies happen when that energy gets tossed out without intention or purpose and the universe treats it like a spell. The bad part about that is that the results are probably not going to be something you'd like to see. When we're in the throes of intense emotion, it's hard to see past that emotion until we calm down a bit. When we do, we usually see clearly that there are better options than simply reaction with no clear intention.

How do we prevent magickal oopsie moments? We ground! Then we breathe, and then we ground some more. Practicing grounding and getting really good at it will help you focus that crazy energy until you really know what you want to do with it. So instead of sending it "up and out" you send it down, into the Earth where it's neutralized and held until you need it purposefully.

Another thing to keep in mind is that as your mind changes, the way you view the world and other people will change a lot too. That's something that happens both during adolescence, and when someone starts practicing a new faith. You're doing both! Your view on ethics and what's important to you now will probably be very different in a year from now. Knowing that your outlook on things is going to change can help you be a little more prepared for it.

Opportunities, not Problems

It may feel like most of this chapter was dedicated to all the problems you'll come up against as you move forward on your teen Wicca path. Although some of these topics can bring up some challenging issues, they really are awesome opportunities if you let them be. The work you do to find teachers, gather learning resources, and deal appropriately with difficult people will set you up to be a wise and mature young person. And as you should know by now, a wise Wiccan is an effective Wiccan. So when you're greeted with challenges, get creative! Trust your intuition, work some magick, and move forward with strength. You can do this!

Chapter 7

Wicca for Life

At this point you should have a basic understand of what you need to do and where you need to look to begin your practice in Wicca. So far we've learned about history, the divine, magick, and how Wiccans practice. In this chapter, we'll look at some of the long-term topics you'll come across as you progress. Many of these things (like daily practice) are extremely important and will be the work of a lifetime. Other issues (like coven and group work) you might not need to think about for a long while.

Wicca is truly a religion for life. What I mean by that is that we don't just show up to practice this religion on Sundays and then forget about it for the rest of the week. The more you practice, the more you'll notice it weaving itself into all these different areas of your life. It's like sand that falls into those little cracks of your life and fills you up, anchoring you down into a rich and fulfilling life. Simply put – you experience every moment of life rather than just let each one pass you by. It's what the Buddhists might call "mindfulness."

Daily Practice

As I mentioned before, Wicca is definitely not a "Sunday religion." There is no single day of the week that you're expected to put the religion pants on to wear around until the end of the day. Instead of having a religious outfit that stays in the closet until its ready to be worn, Wicca asks that you work it into your whole life. Instead of being an outward expression of who you are, it becomes your skin, the air you breathe, and the lungs you use to take in that breath. This is what some Wiccans mean when they say, "Don't *do* magick, *live* magick."

One of the most important ways that we live magick every day is by setting up a daily practice. Think of this like your spiritual exercise routine. You're training to become a stronger, wiser, and deeper spiritual being. Like a muscle, our spirits can be trained to do more.

As you continue along this path, your daily practice and the exercises you do will change pretty frequently, and it should! It's meant to be something that aligns you with the forces of the universe in your day so you can go through that day with better awareness and in better communication with the world around you. As you get more experienced, your daily practice will change to reflect that. Your sitting practice might become a little longer at times or you might have a set of exercises that are more challenging to work on. For now, we can start small.

The fun part about daily practice is that you can shape it however you like. After a while, you'll find a flow that feels right to you. The flow of exercises you do should be consistent, but make sure it doesn't become too rigid. Personally, I like to switch up the flow of what I do once a month. If you end up getting bored with your practice, you won't be likely to stick with it.

Although you can absolutely craft a daily sitting practice based on your own needs, I'll give you a rough outline that you can use to start out. As you learn more and master different techniques, you'll substitute some for others. Your practice will always have some kind of meditation though, as meditation is one of the most important keys to unlocking our spiritual potential.

Example Daily Practice Outline

First Month

1. 5 minutes of relaxation meditation
2. Commune with one element, a new one each day
3. Say a prayer to the Goddess and God
4. Practice moving and directing energy with the hands

Second Month
1. 5 minutes of relaxation meditation
2. Commune with all of the elements
3. Say a prayer to your ancestors and guides in addition to the Goddess and God
4. Practice moving and directing energy
5. Do a short cleansing exercise for the self or your space

Committing to show up for daily spiritual practice might seem like a lot of time you have to spend, but what you get out of it is well worth it. Besides deepening your spiritual connection to the cosmos, you'll find that daily practice will also help you manifest magick faster (and more accurately), increase your intuition, and make tough situations a little easier to deal with. Think of it as a way of fortifying your body daily with superpower vitamins.

Academic Advancement

Although I've tried to give you all the essential information you need to start practicing Wicca, there is obviously way more information that we could jump into on virtually every single topic this book contains. When I asked my first teacher what I could expect once I started studying Wicca, he her response was, "You can expect to read...a lot." She was right! Over the years I've read so many books that nearly every room in the house has an overstuffed book case that threatens to crash to the ground under its own weight. Most Wiccans really enjoy reading because we value the spiritual information from so many traditions – some of which we incorporate into our own.

Just because you'll end up reading a lot of books doesn't mean you have to be an expert scholar on every subject. They key is finding books on topics you find interesting and helpful to your practice. Granted, you won't find every book you read helpful, but you'll always finish one with either a new understanding on something new or a fresh perspective on something old. This is why there are a lot of introductory books on Pagan topics out there. We can all learn awesome new things when we share our unique outlooks on life.

I like to encourage students of Wicca to question everything you learn at some point. That doesn't mean you have to be overly skeptical about everything, but you should come to new information with a mixture of honest curiosity and the heart of a researcher. Take the guardians of the directions for example. We went over their roles a little bit, but where they came from and how they ended up in Wicca is a detailed and interesting story that's worth more research. That research will probably lead you into a deeper understanding of why we call the guardians and what they're meant to do in the circle.

If you really have no interest in a topic you shouldn't feel pressure to learn too much about it, although it's worth it to have a basic understanding. Many Wiccans have a deep love for astrology as that system can be very helpful in learning when the best time is to work the most effective magick. Unfortunately for me, I really hate anything mathematical so anything that requires me to look up charts with degrees and numbers will totally put me to sleep in about five minutes. But still, I got myself a very short introductory book and learned the bare-minimum basics.

The search for knowledge in Wicca, especially when you get into history, can be pretty frustrating. Because Wiccans and other Pagans have such a love for learning, it makes for a lot of opinionated people. Longtime Wiccans have a lot of fun debating different subjects. Debate is good and healthy because it challenges us to learn more, but be careful that you don't get too pushy with things. Remember: even those of us who have been Wiccan for our entire lives remain students. We are forever searching and learning.

Developing the Spiritual Current

Intuition, divine guidance, and "knowledge and conversation with the higher-self" all describe what I like to call the spiritual current. The current is a web of energy that connects all things on this planet and across the universe. It's what allows energy we send from our own bodies to reach the bodies of other people. It's how magick is possible, accessible, and a natural part of reality. The Northern European traditions call it the Web of Wyrd, the threads that connect the fate of all humanity, spun by the goddesses of destiny.

Whenever you've had a gut instinct you followed or experienced a flash of insight or inspiration, you've touched on that current. When fully living the Wiccan life, you'll step into the flow of that current more and more. Daily practice helps keep us there while things like sabbat and moon rituals help us determine the direction our current is flowing in. Part of the reason why we honor the seasonal cycles is to align us with the environment around us, which helps us discern where we're going in life. It also opens us up to greater amounts of energy, and who couldn't use more of that?

I like to imagine the current as a river, flowing endlessly in every direction. Different streams flow above me, below me, behind me, and (most importantly) through me. Sensing which of these streams has a stronger pull can help us with things like decision-making, accessing more energy, and developing psychic intuition.

Exercise – Sensing the Current

Stand in a place where you have plenty of room to move in any direction. As you begin to breathe deeply and drop into a meditative state, imagine the streams of the current all around you. They might appear as a liquid quicksilver or as streams of a muddy creek. However you imagine them, see them as clearly as you can in your mind's eye.

Take notice of the direction the streams are moving in. Do they seem to be flowing mostly in the same direction? Different directions? Is the speed and strength of one stream stronger than the others? Sense that strong current and adjust your body until that stream is flowing right through you. If the stream was above you, you can "call it down" with your imagination.

Gently walk a few steps towards the direction of that current. What does that feel like? If you can sense anything in the distance where the stream is headed, what is it? It might be the answer to an important question, a path to greater spiritual connection, or a compass pointing in the direction of an element that is calling to you. Whatever that is, feel what it's like to stand in the current of where that's going.

Finding Community

If you end up like a lot of Wiccans today, you might find that following your spiritual current means seeking out community. For many, being surrounded by friends and companions who have similar spiritual tastes is absolutely essential. After all, human beings are social creatures. It's a natural desire to feel the need to belong, to have people around us who give us the space to let our unique personalities shine through.

As I write this, the Pagan community across my own country (and certainly the whole world) is experiencing an explosion of growth. What used to be pockets of people in cities and other open-minded areas has turned into something that's practiced in every city in America. Many towns have all sorts of Pagan groups. In my own city of Washington, D.C., you can find groups of Wiccans, witches, Heathens, Hellenic Polytheists, Thelemites, Druids, Celtic Reconstructionists, and more. Granted, I live in a very large city that's grown its Pagan community quickly over a period of decades. Still, that seems to be the direction that many areas are heading in.

Connecting with the larger Pagan community can be really

exciting when you first get into it. My first experience was going to a public ritual held by an adult teaching coven that partially trained me. Although I was shy, I was in a state of total bliss, happily soaking up the conversation of all the adult Pagans around me. It made me feel like I was finally in the company of people who could understand me and what I wanted to do with my life. Being around other people who seem to "get" you is always a nice feeling.

Like any community, the Pagan community has its fair share of problems and one of those problems is reverse-ageism. Traditional ageism consists of preconceptions and discrimination to older individuals. The older folks are seen as less-capable, obsolete, or behind the times. Reverse-ageism is the other way around, ageism against younger people. Most Pagan communities have no problem respecting elders, but respecting youth is a bit of an issue. I'll use myself as an example. As I write this, I'm twenty-five years old and have been walking this path for most of my life. Yet I still go to festivals and events where people who are twice my age (but have been practicing for only a few years) take my ideas and contributions with a grain of salt.

Things are changing though. I'm now seeing more young people than ever before step up to offer really wonderful things to the community. Young Wiccans are going into priesthood training early and spending a lot of time growing their spiritual interests. The older Pagan generations are recognizing that too. So if you have a local Pagan community around you, just go into it with an open heart and an open mind. Be ready to learn but be confident in sharing your thoughts. Everyone has worthy talents to bring to the table, and that includes you!

Working in a Group: Covens and Circles

When talking about finding community, I mostly meant social community. The next type of community goes a layer deeper. A coven is a close-knit spiritual community that many Wiccans participate in for a whole bunch of reasons. Covens provide practitioners with a safe and consistent environment to learn and practice in. Over time, the coven becomes a type of chosen family, which is why you'll often see covenmates call each other names like "brother" and "sister."

Although different covens have different missions and ways of operating, most of them involve meeting regularly to celebrate the turning of the seasons and the shifting lunar cycles. My own coven meets for each full moon and hosts open community rituals for most of the sabbats. Other covens might meet just on the full moon or even on the full and new moons. Meetings can involve discussing business matters such as the acceptance of new members, the state of current members, and plans for future goals and events. Ritual will often be after business meetings and can be pretty similar to the ritual done on one's own. The difference of course is that there are more people involved to share roles. Covens will usually have members assigned to call the quarters, invoke the gods (usually a High Priest or High Priestess), and send out the raised energy.

The advantages of working with a coven can be very appealing, which is why it was nearly a requirement that all Wiccans have membership in one back in the early days of the religion. The first advantage – the added energy that everyone gets to work with – is a major perk. If you remember how magick is partly dependent on how much energy you can raise, imagine how effective it can be when three, five, and even thirteen people are working on the same goal at the same time. Over time, the "hive mind" of the group grows stronger, which increases the coven's ability to raise more energy.

A coven can also provide people with a family-like bond, creating deep friendships that can survive hardships that would crumble many other friendships. But like any family, coveners still bicker and fight with each other on occasion. The close bonds of the coven can be a challenge for a member who isn't meant to have that in their life for the time-being, which can cause a strain on the whole group. Sometimes the strain becomes too much and a member will leave, and sometimes the coven breaks apart entirely. From what I've seen, most covens have an average lifespan of five years at the max. I also know of covens that have been around for nearly twenty-five years. The length of time a coven exists isn't as important as the work that's being done within one. If you find yourself in a coven, there will be times when you find it helpful and times when you find it a challenge. If it's constantly more of a challenge than helpful, then that might be a sign that it's time to say goodbye.

Finding an existing coven to join can be a little tricky for teens. Every adult coven I've ever encountered has an eighteen years of age minimum requirement. As I've mentioned before, I was lucky enough to find an adult family-based coven where the members actually had young people my age as children. That meant that I was able to attend open events and then hang out with people my age. We even formed a circle for our own needs at one point. A circle is a group that's a little looser than a coven. They might do all of the same things, but there isn't much need for formal initiations, creeds, etc.

If you're studying Wicca with a group of friends and begin to meet together regularly, forming a circle can be a great way to make everyone feel committed and encouraged along the path. Your circle can be just a study group where you gather to read and discuss topics. If you have the ability to do it, you could also do ritual and meditation in addition to studying. Over time as you learn more about Wicca and incorporate it into your lives, that circle could form into a coven. You'll find more information on how to do that in the recommended reading list at the end of this book.

Your Thriving Life

If Wicca is the path for you, then your life will truly thrive from it. It is hard work and takes a deep commitment, but if it's meant for you then you'll find that the effort is well worth it.

I believe that any religion should cause all areas of your life to thrive, not just the religion part of it. If other areas of your life are still falling behind like your social life, school, and family commitments, then it's time to take a second look at what this path is doing for you. Ask yourself, "Is this what I need in my life right now?" Parts of this path will challenge you in healthy ways for sure, but it should never keep you from accomplishing other life goals. Instead, it should cause you to thrive in every way.

Chapter 8

The Spells

Alright, on to the ꜰ   ʀous ways they
have been projec   ᴀve enjoyed a
longstanding popu   ᴅ books. From
Samantha Stevens   *ed* many years
ago to the wand-wᴀ   ʀ, the appeal of
spellcraft to the mᴀ   ꜱoon.

If you picked uᴘ   ᴀpter, I suggest
reading through th   ᴏ the workings
leading up to this point first. I've placed spellcraft towards the
end for a few reasons that are truly for your own benefit.

Spells are definitely not done in the way that Samantha or
Harry do them. Sure, I'd love to twitch my nose and have all my
chores done, but it just ain't happening. The truth is, spells can be
a lot of work depending on what you're doing. They require a
focused mind, the ability to relax and raise energy, and a
knowledge of why and how what you're doing will work. The
most common misconception with spells is that they're like
recipes, mixing together some ingredients a certain way for a
specific result. Well, that can be part of it, but that's certainly not
the end of it. Honestly, a lot of my friends in my teen years were
attracted to Wicca because of the spells and then later gave it up
once they realized how much work they are.

Your Magickal Ingredients

Each of these spells contains different ingredients that lend
specific energies towards your goal. As we've already covered in
our chapter on magick, each ingredient corresponds to an energy.
I understand that teens tend to have either very limited cash or
no cash at all. I certainly did not have money to buy all sorts of

herbs and stones so I won't assume that you have the ability to do that either. Keeping that in mind, I've tried to keep the ingredients of each spell as simple as possible.

These spells aren't set in stone which is why you should feel free to substitute ingredients as you need to. The appendix of correspondences will help you here, as well as in other sources where you might find spells with challenging ingredients. For example, let's say you come across a prosperity spell that uses the herb cinquefoil. In looking at the list of herbs in the appendix, I can pick out alternative herbs that also bring prosperity. I scan the list to see what we have in Mom's spice cabinet... Success! I grab the jar of basil, a wonderful and common herb for prosperity.

There are a lot of spells out there that involve candles. As we've already talked about, candles might not be the easiest thing for you to obtain. If you're in a no-candle house, just do your best to be creative. Use visualization and energy to conjure up a flame of energy that you use with your other ingredients. If you can get candles but are limited in variety, always go with white if you have to. White is an all-purpose candle and can really be used as a substitute for any other color.

Before You Cast the Spell

How do you know when it's time to cast a spell? Are you properly prepared for what you need to do before and after? The following is a checklist of sorts that will help you make sure your spell is as successful as possible. Keeping these things in mind will give you a better chance of working effective magick and getting the results you want.

Have I done everything I can do in the physical world first?

A spell shouldn't be the first thing you do to solve a problem or obtain a goal. First, exhaust all of your options in the material world, or do a spell along with those actions around the same time. Magick follows the path of least resistance. If you have all your ducks in a row here on the physical plane, your spell will have an easier time manifesting.

Am I prepared mentally and physically?

It's usually best to avoid spellwork when you're angry, depressed, tired, or sick. Spells require energy so if your energy is unbalanced or not present, you won't generate enough juice to get it going.

What is my environment like right now?

Environmental factors like the phase of the moon, the position of the planets, and even the weather can all affect spells. The most common condition to keep in mind is the phases of the moon. Waxing moons are considered more helpful for spells that are intended to grow things or draw things to you. Waning moons are best for spells that involve decreasing things or pushing things away. Sometimes you just need to do a spell and can't wait for the perfect environmental conditions and that's fine. But it is helpful when they line up.

Do I have everything I need?

It's best to keep focused during a spell so you should avoid having to get up and search for things like missing ingredients. Have everything right in front of you, ready to go. Also, do you have things like privacy? Are your bodily needs met like food and water? These things may not seem very important, but they all have subtle effects on how our energy works and transmits into a spell.

What will I follow up with?

Remember, spells work best when performed in combination with physical actions. Do you have a plan of what you'll do in the physical world to further your goal? If you're doing a spell to get your first job, you should submit applications everywhere you can in the same week.

Now that we've covered all of that, we can get to the business of the spells themselves. The spells I've included here are sample workings I've written myself or adopted and changed over the years. If this is your first time working with spells, I suggest sticking to the way each one is done. Once you gain experience, you can make changes that will make them even more effective for yourself.

The spells are sectioned out by category and are alphabetized so you can find them easily.

Abundance/Attraction

Almond Abundance Spell

Draw abundance into your life when you need to have more of something. You might think of that as more money, but this simple spell is meant to draw more of any good thing you desire. That could mean an abundance of friends, joyful experiences, trading cards, or anything else you can think of. Use this spell if you just want "more" in life.

Materials:

Almonds

Lay a big handful of almonds before you and hold your hands a few inches over them. Begin to imagine your life surrounded by everything you desire and more. Project bright gold and green energy into each of the almonds as you say:

By the green and by the gold
abundance in my hands I hold.
Almonds draw all I desire
by earth and air, water and fire.
Health and fortune, luck and more
all these things come to my door.

Take the almonds and push them into the soil around your house until they can't be seen. If you live in an apartment complex, push them into the soil around there. If you live in a big city with no soil at all around you, then stick the almonds into the soil of potted plants around the house or even secretly under the rugs. The enchanted almonds will draw abundance from every corner of the land.

Orange Attraction Charm

This spell is similar to the almond spell above, but makes it a little more portable. This one is especially helpful for busy teens on the go who aren't home that much. You can keep this charm in your backpack, purse, or hanging in your locker at school.

Materials:

1 orange
Thread or string

Peel an orange making the biggest side peels you can. To make it easy, slice it into quarters and pull the bulk of the orange away from the peel after that.

As you eat the orange slices, fill your mind with all things you wish to tract in your life. You might have one thing in particular or there might be a big number of things. Taste the sweetness of the orange and think about how sweet your life will become as these things draw closer to you. Your desires crave the sweetness of the orange too, making you a magnet for them.

Leave the peels out in a sunny place to dry for a few days. Once they're all dry, pick one or a couple to use for your charm. Using a marker, draw two arrows from each side that point to the center, on the inside of the peel. It should look like this: A A

Poke a hole in the edge of the peel and run your string through it, making a loop you can tie. You can hang this small charm anywhere you like or just carry it around with you, around your neck or in a bag.

Binding/Banishing

The Freezer Spell

This is one of the most famous and popular spells known for binding. Even though it's a simple working, it's still very effective so think about how much you need to bind this person. Have you tried all other worldly options to get someone to leave you alone? If so, then proceed with this spell. Since this is a well-known working, there are many variations. Below is my own version of the spell which has served me well for many years.

Materials:

Ziplock bag
Paper
Sugar
Water

Write the person's full name on a square of paper. All around the name, draw the binding rune ISA, which is just a straight, vertical line. Fold the paper up into the tiniest square you can and put it into the bag. Add a few pinches of sugar and fill the bag halfway with water.

Seal the bag and stuff it into the back of the freezer, covering it as best as you can so it's less likely to be disturbed. Then, slam the freezer door shut and yell:

Sweetness of ice holds you still
your harmful actions ensnared by my will
Frozen ponds and lakes and oceans
aid me in this icy potion
Chill out! Chill out! Chill out!

If possible, leave the bag in the freezer as long as the person has to be in your life. If you've sensed that they've totally turned themselves around (bullies sometimes do that as they get older), you can lay the bag out in the sun and let it melt naturally.

Binding Gossip

This is a simple spell that's a little less extreme than the freezer spell. If someone is causing you harm intentionally or unintentionally through gossip but not in any other way, this quick spell will do the trick.

Materials:

Red cord or string

Hold the red cord (which represents the person's tongue and words) and enchant it by saying:

Your tongue, your mouth, your wicked words
are knotted up within this cord

Take the cord with you the next time you expect to be around the person. If it's not someone who usually talks to you directly, get them to talk to you, maybe by asking them a simple question. When they respond, quickly make a simple knot in the cord and tie it tight as they're speaking. The idea is that their voice gets trapped within the knot so they won't be able to spread lies about you as long as you have it. Store the cord someplace safe.

Banishment Petition Spell

I put this banishment spell under the same category as binding because they both deal with taking care of troublesome people. However, banishment is really in a whole different ballpark from binding. This is the type of spell you would do when a binding isn't working for whatever reason, or if the person is doing something so terribly horrific that it would be best if they were just not in your life at all.

Banishment spells can work in all sorts of ways. This one is open-ended, which means several things could happen. Most often, this will compel the person to stay away from you at all costs. It will act as a magick repellent, causing the person to be completely uninterested with you and your life. On the other hand, it might actually make the person go away literally. One of the few times I did this spell was in the case of a bully who was so awful, I was afraid to go to school every day for a little while. A few weeks after I worked this spell, his father got a better job in California and they moved across the country. As you can see, something good happened to take the bully away rather than something bad. Causing something harmful to happen would have fallen in the realm of curses, which is something we don't really want to mess with.

The format of this spell is called "petitioning" and is used for just about any need you could think of. I find it particularly effective for banishment spells.

Materials:

Sheet of paper
Pen
Fireproof container

Write down a short story of what the person has done to you and why you think they need to be banished. Write down both what has happened and how you currently feel. Fold the paper four times and write the person's name all around the folded paper. Hold the folded paper in your hands and imagine the person's face very clearly. Say:

[person's name], I've done all that I can do
and so I take my leave of you
The time has come you cannot stay,
I cast you out this very day!

As paper is consumed by flame,
Only memories remain

Set the paper on fire, making sure it is completely engulfed in flames, safely inside the container. As the paper burns to ash, stare into the flames and chant repeatedly:

Away away, I banish thee away

When the ashes are cool, scatter them in the wind as you say:

With harm to none the spell is done
I seal it up by moon and sun.
So mote it be!

Blessings

Holy Water Blessing

This simple working can be used to bless people, animals, houses, objects, or really anything else you can think of. Extra water can be stored and used for later so you don't have to do the working all over again.

Materials:

Water
Salt

Have a cup or bowl of water before you on your altar with a small pile of salt right next to it. If you can get fancy sea salt, great! But if not, don't worry about it.

With your wand or athame (or your hands if you need to), touch the salt and begin to imagine it glowing with light, pulsating with power. Imagine each grain of salt vibrating and buzzing with energy from the space around you and from your body itself. Trace several pentacles in the air above the salt and say:

I consecrate thee, oh creature of earth
that you may be fit to bless all that you touch
For in the name of the Goddess and God do I bless you and make
you holy

Next, touch the surface of the water just as you did with the salt. See the water come alive as it swirls around, absorbing all the energy you send into it from the space around you and your body itself. Again, trace pentacles above the water and say:

I consecrate thee, oh creature of water
that you may be fit to bless all that you touch
For in the name of the Goddess and God do I bless you and make
you holy

Add a few pinches of salt to the water and stir it up with your finger. Hold the cup of salted water and raise it up. Feel every inch of universe around you awaken and pour into the cup as a bright light. Sense it filling up the water until it can't possibly fit any more.

The water is now blessed and you're ready to put it to use. Simply sprinkle it or smear it across anything you need to bless. I used to bless my pencils with the holy water before taking important tests in school! It might not make the pencil come alive and pick all the right answers for you, but it will help you recall information and memory that you already worked to get. That's just an example, but the possibilities are endless!

Body Blessing

This simple blessing is done using only the power of your mind. This is a great working to do in the morning before you head out to school. The body blessing helps to keep all of your energy bodies healthy and in good working condition. Read through it a few times and practice going through the motions until you have it down.

Stand up straight with your feet about hip-width apart and breathe deeply. Try to sense the energy in and around your body and just notice what's there without judgment. Do you feel tired? Nervous? Energized? Calm?

In one motion, bend forward extending your arms down like you're trying to touch your toes. Using visualization, "pull" energy up from the Earth as you slowly raise your body and arms, bringing it up through your torso and out through the top of your head. With your arms and body now stretching towards the sky, pull down energy from the sky as you bring your hands down, bringing the energy through your torso again and anchoring it into the ground. Say:

Above, below, and in between
I stand in the center as the witch's tree.

You can do all of the above once or several times. I usually get a nice energized feeling after doing it three times in a row. You could also add to this by sprinkling drops of holy water on yourself before and after.

Cleansing

Shower Cleanse Ritual

Cleansing is an important part of any regular Wiccan practice. As we move through our days, we naturally collect bits of "ick" that can sometimes stick to our energy bodies. Keeping ourselves clear of that as much as possible helps our positive energy to move better.

The most basic cleanse may sound obvious – the shower!

Hopefully you should already be bathing on a regular basis, so it's pretty easy to turn that into a magickal act. The core of the shower cleanse is visualization, although you can add more to it. Simply stand under the shower head and imagine that you're standing under a majestic waterfall in an ancient forest. Every drop of water is a bead of light that blesses you as it hits your head and runs down your body.

To give this working a kick, you could carve sacred symbols into a bar of soap while it's dry before you get into the shower. If you use gel soap, pour it into your hand in the shape of a star. You could also turn it into a full-blown rite with candles, incense, and crystals that line the shower wall. But in its most basic form, the shower cleanse packs a big punch on its own.

House Cleanse

Just as the body can collect negative energy, so can your home. Keeping positive energy flowing through your house helps to lighten up the mood, which can lessen the likelihood of family arguments and tensions. It also creates a calmer atmosphere to work in for your magick.

Materials:

Pot of water
Salt
Basil

Fill a pot up with water and add a teaspoon of salt and at least a tablespoon of basil. Turn on the heat and stir it up, imagining that the power of the basil is "activating" and filling the pot with its green energy. Basil is a powerful cleansing herb and promotes friendship. Allow the pot to get hot enough to let off good amounts of steam, but not boiling too much.

Obviously this spell would need to be done in the middle of the family kitchen. If you're not yet out to your parents about your magickal interests, you can just tell them that the scent of steaming basil lifts moods via aromatherapy, which is absolutely true.

Communication

Call Me Spell

Here's a variation of a tried and true spell that teen Wiccans have been using for decades. The Call Me Spell works by sending a psychic "message" to the person you need to contact you, which will pop into their mind as an idea.

Write the person's name on a piece of paper and draw next to it the rune of communication, Ansuz. Ansuz looks like a capital F with the horizontal lines bent slightly downward. Fold up that paper and place it under your phone. If you have a cell phone and it needs to be carried with you, put the paper into the sleeve, case, or cover of the phone. When the person calls you, take the paper out and throw it away. Easy!

Communication Cord Spell

Most arguments and fights come from a lack of communication between the people involved. It's hard to express exactly what we feel without affecting the emotions of another person. When communication brings about tension between you and someone else, use this cord spell to bring healing and strength to your words. The technique of tying knots in cords is a common magickal method.

Materials:

One long cord, preferably yellow or white – colors of communication. You can use anything from yarn, a thick string, rope, or even a shoelace.

Hold the cord in your hand and slowly run it through your

fingers, imagining you and the other person talking kindly and lightheartedly. When you have the image running smoothly through your mind, begin to tie knots into the cord, one-by-one in a row. Say the following as you tie each knot:

I tie knot one, the spell's begun
I tie knot two to bring us truth
I tie knot three for harmony
I tie knot four to heal, restore
I tie knot five, the spell's alive
I tie knot six as the spell is fixed
I tie knot seven, communication is given
I tie knot eight, to clear the slate
I tie knot nine, our speech is pure, whole, divine.
So mote it be.

Keep the cord with you for the first few times you think you'll need to communicate with the other person. After that, store it in a safe place for a while.

Dreams

Dreams are an important part of magick. We use them to help us find the answers to questions, to meet guides in the otherworld, and to explore our spiritual talents. Here are a couple spells to get you started in navigating that world.

Dream Journal Spell

Writing down the dreams you can actually remember is really the best way to encourage your mind to remember future dreams. Keeping a dream journal was one of the most helpful things I did early on in my Wiccan practice and it's something I still do today.

Materials:

Journal or notebook
Art supplies

Lay out the journal and art supplies before you. First, cleanse the materials by waving your hand over them in broad sweeping motions. Say:

Clarity of air brings strength to my art
I cleanse these tools, negativity depart!

Begin to decorate the cover of your journal with the art supplies in any way you like. Make it a representation of who you are. Think about adding sacred dream symbols like spirals, stars, and moons. When you're finished, hold the journal and charge it with bright, blue light as you say:

I charge this tome to help me dream
by rising moon and setting sun
magick flows throughout its seams
each time the day is done.
Goddess guide me in my sleep
open all my eyes
to other worlds I journey deep
and soar above the skies.
Swans of dreamtime gather near
stay close throughout the night
keep away all doubt and fear
until the dawning light.
Past and present, future and more
worlds beyond the knowing
this journal bless and power store
to keep the dreams a'flowing.
So mote it be.

Keep the journal by your bed as a talisman to draw dreams and to help you remember them. Write down the dreams you can recall as soon as you wake up from one (another advantage of keeping it by your bed.)

To Lucid Dream

Lucid dreaming is dreaming with full consciousness. Although there are different kinds of lucid dreams, the most common are those where you are aware that you're dreaming but allow yourself to go with the flow of the dream anyway. Intense lucid dreams allow you to not only be aware of your dreams, but also allow you to manipulate the dream world as well. Being fully aware in a dream will help you remember your dreams and take note of more specific details about them.

Materials:

Lavender in any form
Notecard or piece of paper

Lavender is a dream plant and its power and scent help bring us awareness in dreams. If you can find real lavender flowers, great! If not, use something that's lavender scented like a spray or mist.

Using a marker, write the following on the notecard: *I bring full presence of mind to my dreams tonight. I remain awake as I sleep.*

Next, draw some kind of symbol on the notecard. It can be anything, although something you usually see in your dreams is helpful. I like to use a tree. The idea is that focusing on this symbol before you sleep will help you "wake up" in a lucid state when you see it in the dream world.

Place the notecard under your pillow and sprinkle the lavender over it. If you have some lavender spray or perfume, spray it on the notecard, the pillow, and your body. This will work the same with lotions or oils, too.

If you do have a lucid dream, explore it freely and be open to any signs, symbols, or messages that might be presented to you. If you meet any spirit beings, ask who they are and what significance they have in your life. When you wake up, you'll probably feel a little tired or drowsy. I like to try lucid dreaming on nights when I have the day off the next day.

Focus

Candle Flame Gaze

Focus is very important for any kind of magick. The more focused we are in the mind, the more focused our magick will be. This first focus working is more of an exercise than a spell, although it's very helpful to do right before a spell. If you can't use candles, use an attractive looking stone.

Materials:

One candle

Stare at the flame of the candle while breathing a little slower than normal. As you gaze at the flame, let your vision soften a little, but don't let it get blurry. Like any form of meditation, thoughts will pop into your brain as you do this exercise. That's okay. Acknowledge thoughts that pop up but let them pass out of your main, maintaining focus on the flame.

Practicing this frequently will make it easier and faster for you to enter a state of focus before a magickal working. You could also use this any time when you need better focus. If you're sitting at your desk in school and need focus before a big test, just imagine the candle flame before you and remember how you felt. Focus will flow into your mind and prepare the way for whatever you need to do.

Rosemary Memory Spell

The herb rosemary is well-known as a plant that stimulates and improves brain function, both spiritually and medically. To work this simple spell, whisper these words into some rosemary and tuck it away in your pocket or in a pouch:

Rosemary is for remembrance

If you can find whole sprigs of rosemary in a garden or in the produce section of a grocery store, great! If not, most home spice cabinets will have the loose leaves. Either will work. Carry the enchanted rosemary with you any time you need your memory to be sharp, like studying for a test and then taking it.

Glamour

Glamour is the ancient art of changing the appearance or perception of something. If you read into the lore of the Celtic faery stories, you'll see many examples of glamour used by both the faery and humans races.

Beauty Spell

Beauty really is in the eye of the beholder, including our own. This spell will shift your appearance, but more importantly it will boost your confidence by helping you to recognize your own beautiful qualities.

Materials:

Flower petals
Bowl of clean water

First, bless the bowl of water. If you can make an altar with beautiful decorations like roses, pictures of you when you looked your best, or items that represent beauty to you, great! Bless and charge all of those things too.

Pick up a handful of flower petals and smell them deeply, imagining the scent entering your body and empowering it.

Close your eyes and imagine yourself in whatever you consider to be your most beautiful or handsome state. More than what you look like on the outside, see yourself with a big heart, walking full of grace and kindness. After holding this vision in your mind, sprinkle the flower petals into the bowl of water. Stir the petals around with your fingers gently as you say:

Aphrodite of the sea, grant me beauty for all to see
The petals of the fruitful Earth meet with the gift of the oceans
By earth and water do I conjure my best and brightest self!
So mote it be

Imagine the flowery water glowing with golden light. Your potion is now ready and at this point you can do a lot of things with it. When I do this spell, I like to sprinkle drops of it all over me while I'm still in that sacred space in front of the altar. You could also take out the flower petals and store the water for later, putting it into a spray bottle or even your shampoo bottle!

To Go Unseen

This spell is a variation of a popular spell that's usually described as an "invisibility" spell. But before you get too excited, you should know that the spell doesn't literally make one invisible. If such a thing existed, there would probably be a lot more bank robbers in the world! What it does is allow you to move about unnoticed, so you seem almost "invisible" to the people around you. It falls under the category of glamour because it's causing a shift in the perception of yourself and others around you. You might work this spell if you're walking through a bad part of town at night and would rather not draw attention to yourself. And truth be told, I used to use it to not get called on during gym class. What you do with it is up to you, but just make sure you're not trying to break any laws.

Materials:

One small mirror (the smaller the better)

Enter a meditative state as you hold your little mirror close to your chest, reflective surface facing out. As you breathe deeply, imagine the mirror turning into a spiraling portal with a dense grey fog rolling out of its surface. The fog gathers all around you as the mirror grows larger and stands before your entire body. Chant the following as you continue this visual:

Those without the eyes to see
cannot look upon this scene
Fog so dense, mirror of reflection
let all vision be met with deflection

You can now walk about and do whatever you need to do. Try not to make eye contact with anyone as doing so will immediately break the spell. When you no longer need to go about unseen, imagine the fog around you getting pulled back into the mirror.

Healing

Healing is a massive category in the world of spells. The spells I'll show you here are a few that I think will be most relevant to you and can be easily adapted. Remember that magick should always be accompanied by actions in the physical world. If you fall out of a tree and break your leg, you shouldn't expect a spell alone to heal it. So if you're sick, do yourself a favor and get checked out by a doctor, then work on the magick side of things.

All-Purpose Healing Spell

This spell can be used for virtually all conditions, big or small. The language of the spell is a variation to a healing spell style that's quite common in the southern and Pennsylvania regions of the United States.

Materials:

A dark-colored stone of any type

You can do this with a person seated before you or on yourself. You can also heal someone long distance by using the stone on an image of the person. A full-body photo is best.

Slowly slide the stone across the person's arms, legs, back, and head. As you do this, imagine the health problem being sucked up into the stone, like it's a mini black hole. It might look different depending on what the problem is. When I have a cold, the energy might look like a gross dark-green color. If I'm just removing pain, it will look bright red like the inflammation that causes it. Be open to any impressions you get which you can record in your book of shadows later. As you slide the stone around, say the incantation:

From the bones and to the muscle
From the muscle and to the veins
From the veins and to the blood
From the blood and to the skin
From the skin and through the pores
From the pores and into this stone
May all illness and maladies be pulled away by the healing power
of Earth!
So mote it be!

You can chant the incantation part as many times as you feel are needed, until all of the energy of the problem has left the person's body. Traditionally, when the working is done the stone would be buried far away. I think it's fine to use the stone again as long as its thoroughly cleansed. Run it under the cold water of a faucet for about five minutes and it should be good to go.

Solar Healing Potion

Materials:

Ginger (1 tbs or 1/5 root diced)
Cinnamon (1 tsp ground)
Lemon (sliced in half)
Glass jar or cup

The fun thing about this potion is that its ingredients have long been known both magically and medically to improve vitality and strength in the human body. Ginger, cinnamon, and lemon are all plants associated with the sun.

Pour the right amounts of ginger and cinnamon into your hand and sense their energies. Feel them awakening into life as you enchant them by saying:

Oh blessed solar plants, who live below the Earth and above it
I summon, stir, and conjure you forth.
Awaken for this healing work and lend your gifts to me.

Drop them into the jar or cup and pick up a half of lemon in each hand. Do the same sensing with the lemon as you enchant it by saying:

Oh solar orb that greets the day
Let healing flow and come my way
I rise as the sun rises

Squeeze all the juice out of the lemon into the jar over the cinnamon and ginger then fill it up the rest of the way with hot water. The reason I recommend doing this in a jar is that it's easiest to just put a lid on it and give it a good shake. But a glass will do, just stir well. Leave the jar in direct sunlight for an hour or so. Then give it another good shake and drink it down.

Soap Bar Spell

You might notice that this spell looks a lot like parts of the shower cleanse spell.

Materials:

Bar of soap
Needle, pin, or other carving tool

With your carving tool, engrave clockwise spirals all over the soap. Big spirals or small, either are fine. Try to carve them a bit deep into the soap being careful to not break the bar apart. With all the spirals carved, trace your finger along the lines of each spiral as you imagine cool, green, healing energy flowing into it. Do this until you feel that the bar of soap is pulsing with enough healing power. While tracing the spirals, you might like to say a healing prayer of your own or simply whisper "healing, healing, healing" over and over.

The bar of soap is now ready to be used. You can use it on occasion to give yourself a full-healing cleanse, or just wash your face and hands with it to keep illness away.

Love

If there are an infinite number of healing spells out there, then there are twice as many love spells. Witches have been known since the birth of witchcraft's existence for performing all types of love spells. Wiccans never use magick to force people to fall in love. And besides, who would want love that's fake and forceful anyway? The following spells will increase your loving vibrations and make it more likely that the right person will notice you a little more.

Materials:

Red or pink construction paper
A photo of yourself

Perfume or cologne
Other art supplies as you see fit

Cut out a big heart in the construction paper and glue or tape the photo of yourself onto it.

Hold the heart against your chest and sense the beating of your own heart. In your mind's eye, imagine your heart glowing bright red with energy that shines magnificently through your body, spilling onto the paper. Now stare closely at your picture on the heart as you say:

I love myself
I love all others
I am important and my life has meaning beyond words.
May the love of the Goddess and God flow into this charm and
shine brightly through my heart and eyes
So mote it be.

Now you can decorate the heart however you like. I like to make a collage with things that represent my accomplishments, hopes, and dreams. I stick stickers and draw symbols and characters that make me happy. Finally, spray a shot of perfume on the heart and the spell is complete.

Place the heart in a location where you'll see it often, preferably at the start of your day. Your bathroom mirror would be a great spot if your household situation allows it. This is one of those spells that doesn't obviously look like a spell, so it can easily be placed in full view, even if your family situation dictates you need to be discreet. It's essentially an art project for confidence. If you are in deep need of self-love, simply repeat the incantation words in front of the mirror every morning to add more power to the working.

Relationship Attraction Spell

Here's where we get into the territory of love magick that affects other people. The purpose of this spell is to draw someone into your life who will be right for you at the time. Make sure you don't have a specific person in mind. If there's a particular person you like, try to put them out of your mind for a little bit while you do the spell. It could be that the person you like will be drawn to you, or the universe might have better plans. The important thing is to trust the magick and remember that the gods have been matching people up like this for centuries. They know what they're doing.

Materials:

(There are a lot of plants listed here that you may or may not have in the family spice cabinet or garden. Just use as many as you can find.)

Allspice

Arrowroot

Basil

Chili powder

Honeysuckle

Roses

Thyme

Willow leaves

Two small candles

Pen and paper

Mix all of the plant ingredients together in a bowl. If you have a mortar and pestle, grind them all together. You can also use your hands to break everything up into a powder-like consistency. Sometimes I prefer that method anyway because it makes your hands smell nice and herby until you wash them. At any rate, mix everything together nicely and then set the plant mixture aside.

Now, write out a list of all the qualities you'd like in a

boyfriend or girlfriend. Start with the words "human, male/female (whichever you prefer)" and the age range. And yes, you really should write "human", as silly as it sounds. I know someone who worked a spell like this who forgot to write that and she ended up with a gang of stray cats who wouldn't stop following her around for weeks! Seriously. So be as specific and detailed as you can. It's okay to write out qualities both physical and emotional.

Place the paper in the middle of some flat surface that won't be disturbed for a week, because that's how long it takes to complete this spell. If you think you'll need to pack everything up and tuck it all away at some point within the week, you can actually contain this whole spell within a shoe box or a suitcase. This is a method you can use if you need to keep your workings discreet. Just be careful of flammable materials since we're going to have some fire going on.

Take out the two candles and inscribe your first name on one and a heart on the other. If you can't use candles, use two stones as a substitution. You can draw the name and heart on the stones with a marker. Place the candles or stones on opposite sides of your flat surface, so your paper list will be in the middle.

Pick up the bowl with the herb mix and sift it through your fingers as you infuse it with energy. As you do this, say the first incantation:

I seek all powers from above
by bird and star and shinning sun
to bless me with a newfound love
Who's sweet and kind and lots of fun
Plants be blessed and grant your power
aid me in this work today
as love is summoned on this hour
and graces me upon its way

Pour out the herb mix in a big circle, with the two candles being just inside of it. Light both candles and imagine that the flames coming off the wicks are being drawn to each other like magnets. Stare into the flames and keep that visual going as you say:

Fire of love, the candle's gift
I invite you to my heart
Come to me and please be swift
empowered by this art
So mote it be!

Let the candles burn for a little while and then extinguish the flames. Each night thereafter for seven nights, move the two candles a little closer together and then light them again. By the seventh night, the candles should be touching each other in the center of the circle and on top of your paper list. Just as the flames are drawn closer together over time, so too will a good relationship candidate be brought to you.

Love Shack Charm

When I was in grade school, the hallways in front of the lockers were the main area where my friends and I would hang out before class started. The inside of our lockers were individual expressions of each of us. I made charms like this to keep the magick flowing while I was at school. This charm is a talisman, which means its purpose is to draw something into your life. In this case, that thing is love!

Materials:

Three plants from the Relationship Attraction spell (pick whichever you have available and like)
One pouch or drawstring bag

If you can find one of those reusable tea bags for your pouch, that's typically what I prefer for a charm like this. Those were hard to come by for me as a teen so I would just put my herbs in a paper coffee filter and tie up the ends with a string. You could also cut out a square of fabric, gather up the ends, and tie that together. See, there really is a way around most spell materials! Anyway, let's move on to the spell itself.

Draw or paint a red heart on the pouch and then draw a pentacle on the inside of that. The heart obviously represents love and the pentacle will "activate" the heart's energy to draw that to your talisman.

Mix up your plant materials just as you did in the Relationship Attraction Spell. You don't need to grind them into a full powder for this one, but break them up enough so that their essential oils are released into the air a bit. When you're done mixing, pour it all into your pouch and tie it up. Hold the pouch in your hands as you imagine the heart on it glowing bright red. Charge it with your own energy as you say:

Herbs of love, mix and mingle
come together for this charm
Be as a lighthouse for the heart-space
be as a budding rose turning toward the sun
I charge you, oh talisman of love
and activate your powers from this day forth
until I deem it ended and scatter the plants to the winds
So mote it be

Hang it up on a hook in your locker and you're done! Even if you're not quite ready for a relationship, you'll find that the Love Shack Charm will make your space feel more friendly and inviting. People might start gathering outside your locker for no particular reason at all. When you feel like the charm has served its purpose (or the school year is ending), take it out and toss the herbs into a gust of wind.

Luck

Everyone could use a little luck in their lives. Luck magick has a really long history in the craft. It works by attuning your personal energies to attract the vibrations of positive experience. After a successful luck spell, things will start to happen that look a lot like coincidences, big and small. It might be a dollar bill that you find on the side of the road or winning a ticket to that sold out concert. Or it could just be a long stream of green lights when you're running late driving to school. Luck spells are best used when you feel like you're "down on your luck" and need a little boost to restore the balance.

Rainbow Luck Attunement

This is a basic practice to attune the energies of your body to luck. It's all about visualization so it doesn't require any tools. But if you like, you could burn some green or yellow candles around you while you do this. Sunday at sunrise would be a great time to do this, although you can really do it any time.

Sit comfortably and begin to breathe deeply, getting into a meditative state. Focus on the circulation of breath as it moves up and down through your body touching all the spaces within it. Begin to imagine that your breath is a soft golden light as it travels in and out. As you breathe in, the light enters your body. As you breathe out, the light surrounds the area immediately surrounding you. Continue to do this for several minutes as more golden light gathers within and around you. Tilt your head up to the sky and imagine that the arch of a rainbow is slowly descending and heading in your direction. It's like the rainbow is drawn to the "gold" of your body. It then washes over you as all the colors bathe your body and your space. Sit within the colors of the rainbow and begin to breathe each one in, one by one.

Breath in red, breath out red (the color of love)
Breath in orange, breath out orange (the color of success)

Breath in yellow, breath out yellow (the color of joy)
Breath in green, breath out green (the color of prosperity)
Breath in blue, breath out blue (the color of peace)
Breath in violet, breath out violet (the color of spirituality)
Breath in purple, breath out purple (the color of magick)

Feel all of the colors swirling about within and around you. If it is hard for you to visualize specific colors, just imagine what it might feel like if you could. We're looking for intention here, not crystal-clear HDTV visuals.

After you've sat with the colors for a few minutes, feel the arch of the rainbow pulling back and ascending back into the sky. As you move throughout your day, you'll be doing so with the power of each color of the rainbow built up in your personal energy.

Clover Spell

Four-leaf clovers are obviously pretty famous for their ability to grant luck. What a lot of people don't realize though is that all clovers attract the energy of luck. You might even say that since three is a lucky number, the more common clovers might even be more lucky! This is one of those spells that takes place over a period of days rather than in one sitting.

Materials:

Clovers

Each morning, go outside and pluck a clover from the ground. Bring it to your bed and whisper this little incantation to it:

Clover bring some luck to me
be with me when I rest
Let everything line up for me
and bring me all the best

Place the clover under or near your bed. Repeat this six more times for a total of seven days and seven clovers. After the seventh day, you can leave the clovers where they are or put them into a little bag to carry with you. The idea is that while you sleep, the magick clovers "reset" the energies in your body to align them with luck and fortune, similarly to the rainbow attunement.

Money

Here's another area of magick that has thousands upon thousands of spells in its corner. Just like love, money has long been a very important part of people's lives since society largely moved away from growing and grazing and into trading and payment. Generally, most Wiccans just use money magick when they need it. That need is up to you though. While it's unlikely that you have bills to pay right now, you still need money to hang out with friends, buy things like clothes, or to keep up with expensive school extras like yearbooks and graduation robes. Most money spells are pretty simple, as you'll see here.

Money-Jar Spell

This spell is so commonly used that I still have never been able to figure out where it comes from exactly. All I know is that it's been around for a while and it works well. There are a few variations to it but this one is my favorite. This spell is best started when the moon is new or there is a tiny sliver of moon beginning to grow in the sky.

Materials:

Medium to large size jar
Art supplies
Coins of any denomination

First, decorate your jar with symbols and images that make you think of prosperity. You might use green markers to draw dollar signs, gold glitter-glue to paint coins, or even paste on pictures of credit cards, banks, and wealthy images from magazines and catalogs.

Take a small handful of change and slowly drop each coin into the jar. Imagine that as the coins it the bottom, each one explodes into large denominations of bills like fifty-dollar and one-hundred-dollar bills. Every day, take at least one coin and drop it into that jar with that visual. This is an ongoing spell that you can keep up with for as long as you like because it ensures that a constant stream of prosperity is flowing towards you. If you do it for so long that the jar becomes full, exchange all the coins for bills at one of those coin-exchange machines. You can then start over with the same jar.

Basic Money Candle Spell

This spell is for a time when you need a specific amount of money.

Materials:

Green candle (a small votive works best for this)

Carve a small pentacle on one side of the candle and the exact amount of money you need on the other side. If you're not sure of the exact amount you need, just round up to whatever you think is your best guess.

Hold the candle in your hands and imagine green energy flowing into the candle. Light the wick and chant the following a few times as you stare into the flame:

[amount you need] or more
cash is flowing to my door

So for example, if I needed $50 it would sound like this: "Fifty dollars or more, cash is flowing to my door."

Let the candle burn all the way down on its own all at once, if you can.

Magickal Tips for Money

There is a lot of lore around money magick that isn't necessarily based in spellcraft. The following is a list of tips and tricks I've learned throughout the years that can draw prosperity to you.

- Try to not make negative statements like "I'm poor" or "I never have money", because that is exactly how you'll stay. Like attracts like.
- Each morning, close your eyes and imagine yourself in your most wealthy state. What do you look like? What type of clothes are you wearing? How much cash do you have in your pocket? Hold the image in your mind before you begin your day.
- Sprinkle pinches of mint and allspice in your wallet or purse.
- Sprinkle crushed cinnamon and cloves around the outside of your home.
- Lay all your money out under the light of the full moon each month so it triples.
- Wear a lot of green and gold colors.
- Always pick up pennies when you see them thanking the universe for the gift and letting it know you are open to all the abundance it will deliver. Never throw change away.
- If you have a choice in the matter, earn money while the moon is waxing and spend it while the moon is waning.
- Jupiter is the planet of growth and expansion. Draw one of Jupiter's symbols in places where you keep money.
- If you garden, plant a few coins in the bottom of the ground and grow the plants above them.
- Ask you spirit guides to go shopping with you. It sounds

silly, but they can help you find some good deals!

Protection

Basic Shielding

Shielding is a core magick technique that every magickal practitioner should know. Keeping up energetic shields helps to strengthen the natural energy bodies that surround us and helps ward away unwanted influences like negative energy, energy suckers, and even danger.

While you are in a meditative state, begin to sense the energy already flowing around you. Bring your awareness to your auric body, that energy that extends about three feet outside of your body in every direction.

In your mind's eye, imagine that energy hardening, as if it's transforming itself from a liquid or gas into a solid. I like to imagine that it's like a watery fluid turning into hard energetic ice. Other times I'll imagine that it's bright golden energy that's crystalizing into an egg of power all around me. Gather energy from the core of your body and push it out into your shields. Gather energy from the space around you and draw it in to strengthen the shields.

Although just doing these visualizations is enough to create a strong energy shield, you can strengthen it even more by adding a prayer or incantation for protection. For example, you might say something like this:

I gird myself with a shining shield of protection
I am guarded and kept safe from all unwanted and unhelpful
influences
By east, south, west, north, above, and below I am protected
By the rising moon, the setting sun, and all the stars in the
heavens I am protected
By my ancestors and the great beloved gods I am protected

By the blessed elements of air, fire, water, and earth am I protected
This shield of protection I charge with my light
So mote it be

Different Wiccans have different views on when you should reenergize your shields. I like to go with whatever my intuition tells me, so sometimes that will be once a week and sometimes that's once a month. If I know I'm going to be in a stressful or risky situation ahead of time, I'll even energize my shields every day if I have to. A couple of times a month is a good place to start though.

Home Wards

A ward is a boundary or wall, so this spell sets a wall of protection around your house. Just like personal shielding, putting up home wards is a standard protective practice in Wicca.
Materials:

Small pebbles
Holy water

Your holy water should already be prepared so we just need to bless and charge the pebbles. If you happen to have access to protective stones like hematite, onyx or obsidian, you can use those. Any stone will work for the purpose of this spell though.

One by one, pick up each pebble and hold it in your hands as you charge it with energy. I like to imagine the energy as blue fire, which is very protective. However you send the energy into the stones, feel that each one is connected to each other by the light you infuse them with.

Next, go outside and place the stones around the boundary of your property. You don't have to recover the stones again so you can push each one into the soil with your thumb, burying it. If you live in an apartment and can't do this, try to place each stone discreetly around the apartment complex. You could tuck each stone into the crevice where the building wall meets the ground if you need to. After the last stone is in the ground, imagine all of them "activating" as they burn bright within the ground. All at once each stone shooting its blue flame up from the soil like a shooting star as it soars up and over your house and down across the other side of the property. It will look like a shining dome of light made out of grid lines that crisscross each other at the top. Do the same visual again, imagining the light going underneath the ground. When you are finished, your home will be in the center of a fiery blue bubble of power.

For the second part, we'll be building up a second line of defense, should anyone or anything bad be silly enough to try and get past your property wards. Take up your holy water and anoint all the doors in your house that lead to the outside. Do the same for your windows, rubbing the water on the outer frames of the window (not the glass). After everything is anointed, stand in the center of your house and imagine the newly anointed doors and windows turning into a golden, liquid light that spreads across all the walls and every surface of your home until everything is shining with bright golden light. Hold your hands up and out like you're pushing something away and say:

I hereby charge and activate these wards of protection!
Protection for my home and all who dwell within it.
Together we are protected from injury, accident, or harm
I call upon the powers of the Earth to awaken and come forth!
Gird this space with your ancient might
So mote it be!

At this point I like to either clap three times or tap my wand on the ground to seal off all the energy, since there will be a lot of it flying about at this point. This is an extremely powerful working so you only need to do it every once in a while. Twice a year and on the solstices are my personal favorite times to do these workings. You don't need to bury more stones though, as long as the original stones have not been uncovered. Rather than redoing that part again, you would just touch the ground outside and "feed" the soil with more of that blue-fire energy. The stones act as a battery while they're in the soil, so they'll absorb Earth energy on their own too.

Magickal Tips for Protection

Humans have always had a very strong interest in spiritually protecting themselves, their families, and their property. Over time a huge collection of protection lore has accumulated. Here's a list of my top suggestions for protective workings that I do myself:

- Charge a necklace or bracelet with fiery blue energy and say a prayer to the Goddess and God for it to become an extra shield for you when you wear it. This is how you make an amulet.
- Sprinkle protective herbs outside the boundaries of your home (you could even do this as part of the warding spell). Common protection herbs include black pepper, rosemary, cayenne, allspice, thyme, and sage.
- Although not a plant, salt is extremely protective when sprinkled around. Try sprinkling pinches of it above door frames and window sills.
- Five-pointed stars are very protective. Draw them on places like the sides of your sneakers, inside your notebooks, or on your skin with a washable marker. They don't have to be big. Big pentagram drawings everywhere might draw unwanted attention.
- Commune with the trees around your home and ask them to lend their protection to the property.
- Carry images of protective animals like crows, bears,

female lions, turtles, and elephants.

- Call on the Goddess in her aspect as the old and wise crone when the moon is new. Ask her for wisdom and protection for the month ahead.

Psychic Power

The ability to tap into intuition and your personal psychic potential is really important in Wicca. Being open to psychic impressions can help us make more informed decisions. It also teaches us the value of listening to what nature and the gods are telling us. And yes, the gods do talk back! We just need to train our ears (and eyes) to receive it.

Awakening the Psychic Fire

Psychic power is usually related to the element of fire. When we train our psychic senses, it almost feels as if a torch has been lit in the darkness. Suddenly we're able to make sense of things all around us that we never knew were there before.

Materials:

One candle of any size or color

Sit in front of the unlit candle and guide yourself into a deep meditative state. Take your time and breathe deeply as you feel yourself relax into the space. As you fall deeper and deeper into meditation, begin to focus on your forehead, in the space that's just a little bit above and between your eyes. Sense the energy that flows into and from that area. This is called the "third eye" chakra, the area where psychic vision manifests. After spending a few moments sensing the energy there, hold your candle and say:

I awaken now to crystal-clear sight
to future, present and past

My vision ignites with the fire inside
the light of this spell that I cast

Light the candle. As you watch the flame grow, imagine that the energy in your third-eye chakra is swirling around, sparking to life like the flame of the candle. Hold the candle close (but at a safe distance) to your face as you sense the light of the fire flowing into your mind, infusing it with power. Visualize this for the span of at least five deep breaths. When you're ready, say:

Within burns a fire
kindled by mind and heart
Strengthen my desire
to see with psychic art
So mote it be

Put the candle down and gaze at the flame again as you meditate for as long as you like. Take your time with the meditation since this is when the psychic energy will "settle" within your body. Extinguish the flame and it's done.

To Bless a Divination Tool

A divination tool could be a deck of tarot cards, a set of rune stones, a pendulum, or anything that helps give you answers.
Materials:

Your wand (use your dominant hand if you don't have a wand)
Your divination tool of choice

On the night of the full moon, take your tool outside or to a window area inside that has a good view of the moon. Set the tool before you and let the light of the moon pour over it. Take some time to meditate with the moon, feeling its power wash over you too. When you feel ready, point your wand at the moon and imagine that a thick stream of bright white light is being drawn from the moon down to the tip of the wand. Pull that energy down and direct it towards your tool. Let the wand touch the tool as the moonlight continues to stream down, meeting the tip of the wand and the surface of your tool. As you do this, say:

Lady of the moonlight, hear my whispered prayer
send your psychic gifts across the midnight air
Let this tool be blessed with visionary power
Let our connection grow with every passing hour

Continuing to draw down the moonlight, trace a triangle around the tool with the energy. The triangle is a symbol of psychic energy and it also contains the energy of whatever is placed inside it. Point the wand into the center of the energy triangle and project energy into it from the wand. Fill up the triangle with energy and fill every inch of the tool. Set the wand down and leave the tool there, allowing it to soak up the remaining energy like a sponge. I like to leave it out under the light of the moon for the whole night and put it away in the morning. Some say that when the divination tool isn't in use, it should be wrapped in a black cloth to keep the energy inside.

Wisdom

A prime goal within Wicca is to become wise. Wisdom isn't something that you can just learn about and have. First you have to get knowledge. When knowledge is put into practice, the experiences you gain from that eventually deepen into wisdom. But even though wisdom has to be experienced, you can use magick to help you to grow wisdom over time. Wisdom magick can help you have a deeper understanding of experiences when they occur.

Owl Spell

Owls have always been the messengers and bringers of wisdom throughout many cultures. They are associated with Athena, the Greek goddess of wisdom who protected the Greek city of Athens.

This spell is really simple. First, find any image of an owl. This can be a magazine or book cut-out, a statue, or really anything. If you're a talented artist (I am not) you could even draw or paint your own owl. Once you get your owl imagine, store it away until the next new moon, when there is no visible moon in the sky.

On the new moon, put your owl on the altar and close your eyes as you fall into a meditative state. Call up the image of the owl in your mind's eye and see it come to life before you. Imagine your owl flying around you with its big majestic wings, as if it were a part of your own spirit. As you breathe, imagine that your breath is matching the pace of the owl. Your two hearts are beating as one. Sit with this image for a while and then imagine owl landing gentle on your shoulder, nuzzling into your neck for warmth. Eventually, the owl turns into pure transparent energy and flows into your body through the pores of your skin. You feel yourself become warm with the fierce wisdom of the owl's spirit.

Open your eyes as you come out of meditation. Look at the image of the owl and bow before it out of respect. You might also say a prayer to the spirit of owl or make an offering of incense if you like. Keep the owl image in some special place where you can see it frequently.

Key Talisman

The key is a symbol of knowledge and wisdom. It opens the door to new experiences. This spell uses an everyday key as a talisman to help you open the doors to wisdom.

Materials:

Key
String or cord

If you can find one of those neat antique skeleton keys to use for this, great! If not, any normal house or padlock key will work fine. A lot of people have keys on their key chains that they don't use anymore, so just ask around and you should find one. The string can be of any kind but should be strong enough to withstand a bit of pressure without breaking. So sewing thread wouldn't be good for this.

Tie your key to the cord and hold it in your hands. Charge the key with energy that flows out of your hands as you say:

I seek the keys of wisdom!
Let the gates of knowledge and understanding be open for me for I
am a seeker of the Wiccan mysteries.
I hold the memories of my ancestors and of the great Wiccan
teachers before me.
I bless this key, that it may grant me access to the halls of wisdom.
May the doors be open, may the doors be open, may the doors be
open.

Hold the key by the cord and slowly swing it around before you, making circles in the air in front of you. Swing the key faster and faster, imagining that a circular portal of energy is opening up before you. As the portal opens, feel the energy of wisdom flow from it and into your mind and heart. Keep swinging the key and holding the visualization for as long as you like. As you slow the swinging of the key, see the portal closing before you.

You can repeat the spell anytime you like, starting with the incantation and following through with pulling in the wisdom energy. You can keep the key as a token on your altar space or hold it with you, maybe as a necklace.

Chapter 9

Rituals

This chapter contains ten basic solitary rituals. The first eight are for the sabbat celebrations; two solstices, two equinoxes, and the four days between. The ninth ritual is an esbat, a full-moon celebration. The final ritual is a self-dedication rite that you can perform whenever you feel the time is right. These rituals are designed to be basic with minimal materials, but feel free to expand on them and add things in. Rituals are most effective when you add your own creativity and inspirations to them!

Yule – Winter Solstice

Materials:

One candle
Cup of juice (orange juice is excellent for this)

This is the first day since the summer solstice that the daylight is finally beginning to grow again. For the ancient people, Yule was special because having more light in the day was important for all things to live. This ritual will feel really powerful if you can do it at sunrise on the morning of Yule. Sit in meditation and think about how your life has been throughout the fall time, the dark time. Feel the sense of hope and anticipation that's in the air as the sun rises above the horizon. What inspires you? What makes you wake up in the morning? Reflect on all of this for a few moments and then light the candle and say:

I greet the dawn of the season! Welcome new sun, who rises up on this new day. I greet you with love in my heart. Although the Earth is falling into the chilled time of winter, I have faith, for I know that the sun will rise again.

Stare at the flame and know that this fire is the same fire as the sun rising before you. Feel the morning light wash over your face and fill you with fresh energy. Take up your cup of juice and let some of that energy flow into the cup. Raise the cup up to the sun for a toast as you say:

> *Oh, young Sun God, I greet you this blessed morning! I celebrate your birth and thank you for your presence. You are the child of promise, born again each year throughout my life and for countless lifetimes before mine. Because of you, I carry the light of the universe within my body, heart, and soul. Blessed be.*

Drink the juice slowly, feeling its power flow into your body. If you like, save a little and pour the rest out on the ground outside as an offering to the land.

Imbolc — February 2

Materials:

Bowl of snow or ice (filled half-way)
Hot water
Pen and paper

Imbolc marks the midway point between winter and spring. Depending on where you live, you might start to see the beginnings of young plants coming up from the icy ground. Imbolc is a celebration of hope and renewal. As the ice melts, it refreshes the land and cleanses us of all the muck of the past dark months.

Write down on your paper all the things you wish to be cleansed of. It could be bad habits, sad memories that bring you pain, feelings of anger, or anything that you feel holds you back. Once you have all of it down, stick it into the middle of the ice, which can be snow from outside or ice from your freezer if you don't have any snow. Put your hands on the ice and feel the power of the Goddess flow into you, warming your hands and pouring heat into the bowl. Say:

I greet you, oh happy maiden Goddess! Although the grip of winter holds us tight, we celebrate the promise of the coming spring. You change everything you touch, melting the ice from our hearts, allowing us to move forward renewed. Goddess, please cleanse me of everything that holds me back. May I greet this season renewed.

Pour the hot water into the bowl and watch as it immediately melts some of the ice and snow. Know in your heart that these difficult things buried within the ice are also melting, softening, and freeing you. Sprinkle some of this new magickal water on your face and body. This is a powerful cleansing potion, transforming all of those nasty things into helpful things. When you're done with it, pour the rest of the water onto the ground. If you have some early-spring plants coming up, pour it over the plants as an offering.

Ostara – Spring Equinox

I like to think of Ostara as the time when everything is "waking up." In my area, the end of March is when it looks like everything around me in the natural world is bursting into life. This ritual will attune you to Ostara by "waking up" the Earth energies.
Materials:

Instrument of your choice. Make one if you need to, like pots for drums or paper plate rattles.
Wild flowers

Take a walk and look for some spring flowers, even if you only have access to "weedy" flowers like dandelions. Take your time and make the walk a sacred act, singing and humming as you go. Ask each flower for permission before you pluck it out and use your intuition to sense if it's okay. This is polite harvesting. Once you have a handful, take them back to your altar and set up your ritual space as usual.

Hold the flowers up to your face and deeply smell them, imagining that your own spirit is mingling with the energy of the flowers. Think about how these flowers had to take a long journey from seed to sprout before finally blooming into a lovely spring flower. This is a lot like your journey, a sometimes-rough adventure that eventually blooms into something beautiful.

Lay the flowers on the altar and take up your instrument. At this point I should mention that if you can't make noise where you are for whatever reason (like a college dorm), you can quietly clap your hands. Start playing a beat on your instrument as you meditate on the spring energy around you, imagining that your song is waking up the Earth. Sing any joyous song you like that gets you moving.

When you're done with your little jam session, take the flowers back outside and scatter them in all four directions outside of your house. This will "plant" good energy into the area around you that will grow for the rest of the season.

Beltane – May I

Beltane is all about the union of opposites, the coming together of things that seem different but end up working together in harmony anyway. This union (the marriage of the Goddess and God in Wiccan belief) brings fertility and abundance to the land. This ritual will unite the different parts of your own self and bring some more abundance to your life. Who couldn't use more abundance?

Materials:

Three strands of ribbon or cord

First, make a list that's separated into two columns. On one column, write out all the things that you don't particularly like about yourself right now. It can be anything from physical features, fears you have, guilt from the past, anything. On the other column, write all the things you love about yourself. What are you proud of? What brings you joy and hope? Once your list is done, sit and meditate on the things in each column. Hold both sides in your mind without judgment. Know that nothing on this list is "bad" in this moment, just opposite of one another. What would it look like if the things you like blended and merged with the things you didn't like? Many mystics believe that this is what enlightenment is – the acknowledgement and empowerment of all these different sides of ourselves.

Take your three strands of ribbon and start to braid them together, still thinking about everything on your list coming together. If you'd like to chant while doing this, you can say:

All of me is fused with power
I celebrate this Beltane hour

Once your braid is done, tie it to your wrist like a bracelet or to your ankle. Let it be a reminder of your commitment to accept and empower every part of you. On this path, every part of you is worthy, loved, and powerful!

Litha – Summer Solstice

Litha marks the height of the power of the God, represented by the sun. This day is considered to be very powerful for magick of all kinds for this reason. It is also one of the days that the veils between our world and the world of the nature spirits is said to be thin. This ritual will help you commune with all of those energies.

Materials:

Your wand
A small offering

This ritual is best performed at the height of the noon day. Any time where the sun is out is fine though. If the sun is shining, position yourself so the light of it falls on your face and space. Feel the sun wash over you, sinking into your skin and filling you with power. Raise your wand and point it at the sun (but don't stare at the sun!) and draw in the sun's power through the wand and into your body. Say:

I greet the height of summer! Oh great God, you dance across the earth ablaze with fiery joy and strength. Help me to also recognize my own strength. As the sun shines brightly on this first day of summer, I attune myself with the powers of the light.

Continue to pull in solar energy until you feel like you can't hold any more. When you're ready, take out your small offering (food or drink is best) and lay it at the base of a tree or by some running water. As you do so, make a prayer of thanks to the spirits of nature. Send them a blessing on this day and they might just return the favor.

Lughnassadh – August 2

Lughnassadh is the first harvest, a time where all our skills and talents are needed to reap the full benefits of what we've planted earlier in the year. This ritual will attune you to this energy and open you to your own special gifts.

Materials:

Pen and paper
Oil

Prepare your ritual space and begin to meditate on the meaning of this day and how you relate to it. What are your skills, gifts, and special talents? What sets you apart from others in your family or school? It might be something obvious like a talent with math, or something subtle like the ability to write a poem or to smell rain before an unexpected storm. As things come to mind, write them down in a list on your paper or in your journal. Think about each one and how important you are in the world because of it.

Now it's time to bless the oil which we'll use to bless our bodies and awaken those gifts to full potential. The oil can be any oil that's safe for the skin like sunflower, almond, or peanut oil. You can even use basic vegetable oil if you need to. If you happen to have access to some sweet-smelling essential oils, you can add a few drops of that to your main oil base. Oil is used often in Wicca to anoint the body. The anointing transfers blessings and marks us as sacred. Hold the container in your hands and say:

> *I celebrate the first harvest with a show of skill! This body is my own. These gifts are my own. My hands shape my own future and the world before me. I embody the strengths of my ancestors. I dance in the joy of the God, who slows and prepares for rest. My hands reap what they sow, and what they sow is always a blessing, always a blessing, always a blessing.*

Continue to softly chant "always a blessing" as you anoint yourself with the oil all over. Imagine your skin glowing with golden light, like a new sun slowly waking up. Think about your list as you do this. Throughout the day, look at your list a few times and remember how strong you are. You may even remember more skills that should be added. Go ahead and add them.

Celebrating Lughnassadh does a couple of things that are very important when you're young. First, it encourages you to recognize how awesome you are, no matter who you are! That confidence is so important as you move forward in life. Second, it helps us remember that what we reap is what we sow. In other words, we generally get out of the world what we put into it.

Mabon – Autumn Equinox

Since Lughnassadh is the first harvest, that makes Mabon the second. Mabon is the time of great abundance, when we look at all of the good parts of our life (even if they're few and hard to see) and give thanks. Think of it like a Wiccan Thanksgiving. I love this ritual because it's simple but powerful, connecting directly with the power of nature and the fall season.

Materials:

Fallen leaves

Go on a hunt for fallen leaves. Pick up ones that call out to you, either by their color or shape or based on a particular type of tree that you like. You'll want to get at least a couple dozen.

With leaves collected, go find an area outside where you can sit undisturbed. If you live in a big city with no park or just can't get outside for some reason, you can do this indoors if you need to. Try to have your window open if you're inside though. The point here is to really feel the essence of the autumn season around you.

Take your leaves and arrange them evenly in a circle around you. If it's a windy day, it might help to put a small stone on top of each one to weight them down. But it's okay if some of them blow away. Once your leaves are around you, sit in meditation for a while, taking time to sense the power of the season. What does autumn in your area smell like? What does it sound like? Are there any particular animals running or flying about that are unique in this season? Think about those things as you sense earth beneath you humming with power.

Look at the leaf directly in front of it and name it for something that you feel grateful for. It might be one word or it might be a whole story that you attach to the leaf. Turn your body around the circle and do the same thing for each leaf. Once you get back to the first leaf, take a few deep breaths and think about all of those things you just mentioned being thankful for. In your heart, know that these things are a part of your life because of your own doing and the gifts of the gods, all combined. When you feel ready, say:

At this time of autumn, I make my gratitude known. My thanks fall upon the heart of the Lord and Lady as the autumn leaves touch the cooling ground. I open my life to abundance as I give thanks for what I have and what is to come. Even in this time of growing darkness, I know that I am rich in body and soul. Blessed be.

Go back to meditating on your gratitude and then leave the space whenever you're ready. This is a ritual that works well with others too. Each person can take turns naming a leaf for something they're grateful for. When I do this with friends, we also like to bring a picnic lunch with us. Feasting and celebrating is a great way to connect with the power of Mabon. Recognizing all that you have will open you up to great things to come.

Samhain – October 31

Samhain is the time when we honor the God as he dies for the season until Yule. It's also the time when we honor our ancestors and all of our deceased loved ones who have come before. This ritual is based on both of those themes.

Materials:

One candle
Cup of water

This ritual is best done either at sunset or at night, since Samhain is the time of darkness and endings. Find some quiet place where there's not much else going on in the background. After you set up your circle space, breathe deeply and focus your thoughts on the night around you. Once you feel connected to the energy of the night, raise your arms up and call out to the Goddess and God:

Oh Great Goddess, on this night you are the weaver
cutting the threads of life so we can live again.
You are the grandmother of time
giving us comfort at the time of rest.
You are the dancer of the stars
shining hope upon us until the light returns again.
Oh Great God, on this night you leave us
traveling to the land of the dead.
Through the western gate you depart
to the place of memory and timelessness.
You are the Bright One
dimming your light for a time as the Earth goes to sleep.
You are the Old One
our grandfather of all who have come before.
Goddess of the night, God of the shining sun, I give you honor and
thanks on this Samhain night.
Blessed be.

Light your candle if you have one, or imagine a small flame glowing before you. Let your thoughts turn to the memory of people in your life who have died, however long ago. If you can't think of anyone and haven't experienced the death of a loved one yet, just focus on the idea of your ancestors. You don't have to know who your ancestors were to honor them. As you meditate on your ancestors, you might even think of a face or name that will randomly pop up in your mind. Make a note of what you sense because it could very well be a departed ancestor saying hello! Being in your cast circle is important here because it makes sure that no creepy unknown spirits reach out to say hello.

Now we'll honor each of those people by pouring water for their memory. This is a longstanding tradition borrowed from many cultures around the world, particularly the African diaspora. If you're outdoors, you can pour the water directly into the ground. If you have to do your rituals inside, you can pour it into a big bowl and then toss the water later. Focus your attention on the memories of each person you'd like to honor. For each person, pour out some water and say "I thank you and bless you" each time.

After this, some people will try to commune with the spirit energy of their loved ones. At my house, we all make a special dinner with foods that our dead loved ones enjoyed in life. We all eat the meal in silence. That's called a "dumb supper" and it's one of my favorite traditions. Try that or develop traditions on your own. What can you do to honor the dying God and the people who have come before you?

Esbat (Full Moon) Ritual

Just as the God reaches the very height of his strength and power on Litha, so does the Goddess reach this same height on the full moon every month. Wiccans commune with the energy of the full moon for greater personal power, using it to add extra energy to spells and prayers. My first teacher used to tell me that any magick performed on the full moon would be at least three times more powerful than any other day. This ritual is based on a common full-moon ritual structure that many Wiccans use every month. This ritual can be performed whether or not you can see the moon (being indoors or in bad weather could make the moon unseen for you) but it's nice if you can have a view of the moon.

Materials:

Wand
Small bowl of water

Set up your ritual space as usual and then sit in meditation for a few moments, sensing what your own energy feels like right now. If you have candles and incense you can go ahead and light those now. Sense how the environment around you feels. Do you notice how the air feels like it's buzzing with power? Or maybe you notice the call of animals in the distance?

When you feel prepared, raise your arms up, pointing your wand right at the moon if you can see it. Imagine that the bright light of the moon is streaming down from space and entering the tip of your wand, which then fills your whole body and spills out into your circle space. Breathe this powerful moonlight in, allowing it to enter every pore of your skin. When you feel full with moonlight, recite the Charge of the Goddess (see chapter 2).

Point your wand at the bowl of water and draw the light of the moon down once again, but this time into the water itself. The water shines bright with power until it can hold no more and fades into a gentle blue and white glow. Pick up the cup and say:

By the power of full moon bright
I call the Goddess on this night
Great Lady of the midnight hour
I seek to know my inner power
May my life be filled with desire
and blessed be earth, air, water, and fire
My body, heart, and soul are shown
each day you make your presence known
So let my every wish come true
Great Goddess do I ask of you

Anoint yourself all over with the water. Sprinkle drops of it around your space too. When you're done, you can sit in meditation staring up at the moon. If you like, you can add other magickal work to the ritual after your main esbat ritual. Many Wiccans will also give a small offering of a cake and some liquid drink that you also eat some of yourself. The great thing about the esbat ritual is that it can be (and has been) changed and played around with based on your own unique creativity. The Goddess is the power of creativity that lives in the heart, let that speak through your ritual.

Self-Dedication

So you've been practicing frequently, studying as much as you can, and have developed a meaningful relationship with the elements, the Goddess, and God. What's next? If you've come to a point in your training where you feel like this might be the path for you for a while, you may decide to self-dedicate. A dedication ritual lets the gods know that you're serious about your religious studies and wish to walk the Wiccan path "officially", at least for a time. It also connects you to a greater flow of energy and power, which can help guide you along your journey.

This ritual has a vow in it. Vows and oaths are very important in Wiccan dedication and initiation rituals. This vow is pretty basic and helps to affirm what you really want out of the Wiccan path. Feel free to add things into that vow as you like, as long as you're sure you can keep up with the promise.

Materials:

A trinket to represent your path (necklace, bracelet, ring, a charm, etc.)
Anointing oil (scented is best but just plain olive oil is fine too)

Set up your altar and ritual space in the usual way. Cast the circle, call the four guardians, and invite the Goddess and God to join you in your space. With everything prepared and your materials before you, sit in meditation and reflect on what you've done in terms of Wiccan practice up until this point. How has it helped you? In what ways did it challenge you and help you grow into a better person? How have you changed from all of this? You may like to record this in your personal journal.

When you're done reflecting, hold out your hands before you, palms facing up, like you're about to hand someone something. This is a devotional gesture that shows you're giving an offering. In this case, your dedication to the path is your offering. Take a few deep breaths and then say:

Gracious Mother, Gracious Father
Hear my words that drift upon this enchanted air
I sit before the altar of the Wiccan ways and ask for your blessing
Make me pure in heart and mind, with love guiding my every action
By earth and air and water and fire
By the strength of spirit and the circle of life
I make my intention known.

Trace a pentacle over your anointing oil. Dab the oil on each part of you as you say each part of the following:

Blessed be my feet that have brought me to this path
Blessed be my ankles that hold me up so strong
Blessed be my knees that help me move with the flow of life
Blessed be my belly that holds my sacred breath
Blessed be my heart that beats with the love of the all
Blessed be my neck that connects my heart and mind
Blessed be my lips that speak only words of truth
Blessed be my head that's filled with wonder and brilliance

Fully anointed and blessed, hold out your hands, palms up again, and prepare to speak your vow. Remember that you can change these words but just have your version prepared ahead of time so you can say them with certainty and confidence. When you're ready, speak your vow:

I [say your name], on the day of my dedication do pledge this vow:

I will listen to the voice of the Goddess and God, within nature and within my own heart.
I will show love for the Earth and all living creatures within it.
I will observe the cycles of the seasons on the wheel of the year.
I will speak my desires to the ever-changing moon.
I will speak words of truth.
I will act with honor and respect to all I encounter.
I will love my body and treat it kindly.
I will engage my mind and always strive to learn.
I will meditate and seek peace within and without.
I will stand in strength and power.
I will move with compassion and empathy.
I will use the power for the highest good.
I will harm none.
I affirm that I will keep these vows unless I find that my journey leads me away from this path.
So mote it be.

Take up your piece of jewelry or trinket that will represent your path moving forward. Place it on you or near you as you say:

In the presence of the Goddess and God
In the company of the elements and the magick all around me
I dedicate myself to the Wiccan ways
May this token be a reminder of my sacred vows
May I move forward with strength and purpose
With perfect love and perfect trust.
Blessed be.

Blow a kiss to each direction, including above you and below you (for sky and land). Now would be a great time to feast on those cakes and juice I mentioned in the esbat ritual. Now it's time to celebrate your journey forward as a real and true walker of the Wiccan way.

Conclusion

Whether you picked up this book because you're curious about Wicca or you used it as a manual to begin your own journey down this path, I congratulate you! If you've done the work in this book by celebrating some of the seasons, the moon, and developed a personal spiritual practice, you have a good starting understanding of what it means to be a Wiccan.

But wait, there's more! Like all things, there really is no true end to this. Wiccans are always seeking and always looking to learn more. At 13 years old or 92 years old, the Wiccan path is a journey of self-discovery, empowerment, and communion with all that the world has to offer. Where you go from here is up to you. It's possible that you may decide that Wicca is the right path for you for the rest of your life. It's also possible that you will find another tradition within the big Pagan umbrella of practices that fits you better. Either way, you can expect your spiritual interests to grow and evolve right along with every other part of you.

As you grow in your path, you'll find it really helpful to maintain a daily practice of some kind. What that looks like will change based on the practices and exercises you adopt along the way. As we've already talked about, daily practice is the foundation of developing yourself into a deep and uniquely powerful human being. Whenever I would have a rough time in middle school and high school, I always had my daily Wiccan work to bring me back to a place of love and connection.

Maintaining balance during the tough times is so helpful and that is probably one of the best parts about practicing Wicca as a teen. You will struggle and face challenges, some bigger than others. That is inevitable. But living the Wiccan life will help you remember that no matter what, you are important. No matter what, you have a role to play in this big beautiful world of ours. And no matter what, you are loved beyond imagination.

I truly believe that young people are the key to bringing Wicca and other Pagan traditions into a new age of acceptance and visibility in society today. We're already seeing that acceptance grow by leaps and bounds, but there is still a lot of work to do. The role you play is so important and the work you do as you walk along the path now will bring our religion to places we never thought possible. And all you have to do to make that happen is to live with an open heart and a kind hand.

I wish you so much luck in your journey, wherever it takes you.

Blessed be,

David Salisbury

Appendix I

Correspondences

Correspondences help us understand the natural world better. When we understand the natural world better, we gain a better understanding of how things like energy and magick work. This section of the book contains correspondences that you can use for ritual spells, meditations, and anything else you can think of for your spiritual practice. This is definitely not a complete guide by any means (entire books have been written just on correspondences) but this should give you a good start.

Symbols

Figure 2, Pentacle: As the prime symbols of Wicca, the pentacle represents the five elements of earth, air, fire, water, and spirit. The circle represents either the circle of life or the interconnectedness of all things.

Figure 3, Spiral: One of the oldest sacred symbols known. The spiral represents the cycle of birth, death and rebirth. Spirals drawn clockwise draw energy in while spirals drawn counterclockwise send energy away.

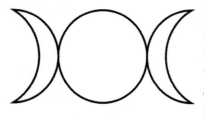

Figure 4, Goddess: There are so many symbols that represent the Goddess and this one is usually considered the main one. The crescent moon on the left represents the maiden, the full moon in the center is the mother, and the crescent on the right is the crone.

Figure 5, God: Similar to the Goddess symbol, the God symbol looks sort of like a stag head with horns, representing the God as lord of all nature.

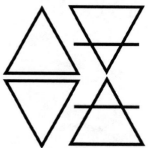

Figure 6, Elements: These are symbols of the elements that come from the magickal system of alchemy. Top left: fire, bottom left: water, bottom right: air, top right: earth.

Figure 7, Triquatera: A Celtic symbol that represents the three realms of land, sea, and sky. It can also represent past, present, and future or above, below, and center.

Figure 8, Eight-Spoked Wheel: A representation of the wheel of the year, each spoke being one of the eight sabbats.

Figure 10, Ankh: This ancient Egyptian symbol is used a lot in many Wiccan traditions. It represents eternal life and the mysteries of the Otherworld.

⊙ ☿ ♀ ⊕ ☾ ♂
♃ ♄ ⛢ ♆ ♇

Planets
(Pictured above from left to right)

Sun: Life, vitality, success, courage, power
Mercury: Communication, change, intelligence, memory,
skill, travel
Venus: Love, beauty, happiness, creativity, friendship
Earth: Grounding, healing, the home, peace, nature
Moon: Intuition, change, magic, wisdom, growth, meditation,
balance
Mars: Action, power, passion, strength, willpower
Jupiter: Discipline, abundance, prosperity, justice, luck,
leadership
Saturn: Binding/banishing, concentration, stability, cleansing,
focus, freedom
Uranus: Insight, illumination, hope, empowerment, goals
Neptune: Dreams, psychic power, protection, guidance, groups
Pluto: Justice, karma, spirituality, major change, life-after-death,
money

Days of the Week
Monday: Dreams, healing, psychic work, truth, family
Tuesday: Action, strong energy, courage, conflict, strength
Wednesday: Communication, self-improvement, travel, wisdom
Thursday: Abundance, leadership, loyalty, success, luck
Friday: Love, beauty, friendship, happiness

Saturday: Binding/banishing, protection, freedom, break-through
Sunday: Attraction, growth, pride, success, ambition

Colors

Black: Binding/banishing, wisdom, protection, endings, the Goddess
Blue: Dreams, emotion, justice, truth, astral travel
Brown: Grounding, growth, rebirth, beginnings
Gold: Success, happiness, increase, prosperity, strength, the God
Gray: Moving between the worlds
Green: Healing, money, harmony, nature
Indigo: Peace, purification, clarity
Orange: Material gain, attraction, joy, support, warmth, the home
Pink: Friendship, calm, compassion, generosity
Purple: Psychic power, blessings, intuition, creativity, spirituality
Red: Protection, love, determination, willpower, focus
Silver: Dreams, psychic power, communication, change, clarity
White: All-purpose color, beginnings, peace, power, protection, manifestation
Yellow: Communication, happiness, knowledge, learning, wishes, skill

Numbers

One: Beginnings, harmony, leadership, individuality
Two: Balance, change, increase, support
Three: Blessings, control, protection, success
Four: Community, the elements, justice, order, stability
Five: Attraction, protection, spirituality, freedom
Six: Affection, comfort, creativity, well-being
Seven: Luck, faith, imagination, love

Eight: Abundance, discipline, patience, success
Nine: Healing, creativity, inspiration, psychic power
Ten: Success, unity, order, power

Animals

Bat: Transformation, insight, goals
Bear: Protection, knowledge, healing
Beaver: Cooperation, motivation, the home
Cat: Dreams, enchantment, power
Coyote: Learning, skill, fun
Crow: Adaption, wisdom, messages
Dear: Peace, clarity, grace
Dog: Devotion, courage, protection, magic
Elephant: Wisdom, patience, strength
Hawk: Awareness, psychic power, skill, omens
Lion: Courage, loyalty, leadership
Monkey: Joy, skill, family
Rat: Cunning, cooperation
Snake: Healing, magic
Tiger: Action, passion, power
Whale: Creativity, memory, support
Wolf: Trust, strength, change, knowledge
Owl: Wisdom, the afterlife

Stones

Agate: Confidence, grounding, luck
Amber: Balance, beauty, manifestation
Amethyst: Psychic power, dreams, inner peace
Bloodstone: Abundance, power, strength
Calcite: Awareness, confidence, creativity
Citrine: Prosperity, joy, clarity
Emerald: Emotional balance, memory, omens
Hematite: Blocks negativity, support, calm
Lapis: Concentration, spiritual growth, truth

Moonstone: Intuition, psychic power, wisdom
Obsidian: Clarity, protection
Onyx: Memories, nightmares, stability
Quartz: All-purpose, power, amplification
Tiger's Eye: Courage, confidence, protection

Herbs

Alfalfa: Money
Allspice: Healing, money
Aloe: Healing, luck
Anise: Protection
Apple: Love
Ash: Protection, power
Balm, Lemon: Success, healing
Bamboo: Luck, breaks spells
Basil: Love, purification, prosperity
Bay (Laurel): Strength, protection, healing, psychic power
Birch: Protection, new beginnings
Blueberry: Protection
Buckwheat: Money
Caraway: Protection (especially of objects), mental power
Cardamon: Love
Cashews: Money
Catnip: Beauty, happiness
Cedar: Purification, new beginnings
Celery: Mental power, psychic power
Chamomile: Sleep, money, peace
Chestnuts: Love
Chickweed: Fidelity
Chili Pepper: Breaks spells, truth
Cinnamon: Success, spirituality, healing, psychic power, love, protection
Cinquefoil: Power, luck, protection
Clove: Protection, money

Clover: Luck, success, money
Coriander: Healing, love
Cumin: Protection, purification
Curry: Protection, change
Daisy: Love
Dandelion: Wishing
Dill: Protection, money
Elm: Love
Eucalyptus: Healing
Fennel: Protection, healing
Fig: Love
Garlic: Protection, healing
Ginger: Success, money, love
Ginseng: Beauty, love, wishing
Grape: Abundance
Hazel: Luck, protection
Holly: Dreams, protection
Honeysuckle: Money, psychic power
Ivy: Protection
Juniper: Protection, purification
Lavender: Love, protection, peace, happiness
Lemon: Friendship, success, stopping gossip
Lemongrass: Psychic power
Lemon Verbena: Love, purification, power
Lime: Healing
Maple: Money, love
Marjoram: Protection, love, happiness, money
Mint: Money, healing, protection (in travel)
Morning Glory: Binding, peace
Mustard: Protection, psychic power
Oak: Protection, power, healing, luck, money, the God
Onion: Protection, absorbs negativity
Orange: Success
Parsley: Protection

Peach: Wishing, love
Pepper: Protection
Peppermint: Healing, psychic power
Raspberry: Protection, love
Rose: Love, friendship, psychic power
Rosemary: Protection, love, psychic power, love, purification, ancestors
Sage: Cleansing, wisdom, wishes, protection
Spearmint: Healing, love, mental power
Sunflower: Success, wishing
Thistle: Strength, protection
Thyme: Healing, purification
Turmeric: Purification
Vanilla: Love, mental power
Violet: Protection, luck, love
Willow: Love, protection, the Goddess
Yarrow: Courage, psychic power, love

Appendix 2

Resources

Recommended Reading

There are so many Wiccan and Pagan books out there that it can feel really overwhelming to pick out ones that will be right for your path. It's important to read as much as you can so you can get different perspectives about things from different authors. My view on Wicca is not everyone's view on Wicca and I hope after reading this book you'll seek out different ideas. The following is a list of books that I think you'll enjoy to help you deepen your journey into Wicca:

21st Century Wicca: A Young Witch's Guide to Living the Magical Life, by Jennifer Hunter
Buckland's Complete Book of Witchcraft, by Raymond Buckland
Wicca for One, by Raymond Buckland
Wicca, by Scott Cunningham
Earth Power, by Scott Cunningham
Wicca for Beginners, by Thea Sabin
The Inner Temple of Witchcraft, by Christopher Penczak
Sons of the Goddess, by Christopher Penczak
The Spiral Dance: A Rebirth of the Ancient Religion of the Great Dance, by Starhawk
Spirited, by Gede Parma
Everyday Magic, by Dorothy Morrison
Power of the Witch, by Laurie Cabot
Encyclopedia of Wicca and Witchcraft, by Raven Grimassi
Wicca: A Year and a Day, by Timothy Roderick
Sabbats, by Edain McCoy

Websites

We've already discussed how it's so important to be careful and wise when looking at resources online. This is a list of websites that have been around for a while and generally have reliable content. Some content on these websites might not be suitable for everyone, so use your best judgment when browsing.

The Witches' Voice: An online resource of Pagan events, organizations, and individuals all over the world – www.witchvox.com

The Pagan Federation: The Pagan Federation is an organization that has been around in the UK for decades – www.paganfed.org

Religious Tolerance: A resource on Wiccan rights and a helpful link to give to family members – www.religioustolerance.org/witchcra.htm

Circle Sanctuary: One of the oldest Wiccan organizations in the United States, Circle Sanctuary is headed by Selena Fox and runs a huge amount of Pagan programs – www.circle sanctuary.org

Patheos Pagan: Patheos is an interfaith blogging website and has a huge section of Pagan blogs to read every day – www.patheos.com/pagan

The Wild Hunt: The Wild Hunt is considered the top source for Pagan news and community information in the United States and abroad – www.wildhunt.org

Life Resources for Teens

Everyone needs help sometimes and there's no shame in seeking out help if you need it. Life can be tough as a teen but I promise you that it does get better. In the meantime, we need you to stay here with us. Here are a few resources that have either helped me personally, or have helped friends of mine.

National Suicide Hotline: 1-800-SUICIDE (784-2433) or the

National Suicide Prevention Lifeline: 1-800-273-TALK (8255). Both are toll-free, 24-hour, confidential hotlines which connect you to a trained counselor at the nearest suicide crisis center.

The Trevor Project: The Trevor Project operates the only nationwide, around-the-clock crisis and suicide prevention helpline for lesbian, gay, bisexual, transgender and questioning (LGBTQ) youth. The Trevor Helpline is available as a resource to parents, family members and friends of young people as well. Visit www.TheTrevorProject.org for more information and resources for young people, including "Dear Trevor," an online Q&A forum for non-time-sensitive questions. You can also call 866-4-U-TREVOR, any time, day or night for help.

Stay Here With Me: This awesome project was started by activist Kelsey Gibb and poet Andrea Gibson, who are friends of mine. The site contains stories and inspiration for youth of all kinds and it's something I wish I had when I was a teen. www.stayherewithme.com

Stop Bullying: A website constructed by the US government that contains resources for bullying awareness and an area where you can report cyber-bullying. www.stopbullying.gov

It Gets Better: A website with hundreds of video testimonials for youths to become empowered and reassured. www.itgets-better.org

Soul Rocks is a fresh list that takes the search for soul and spirit mainstream. Chick-lit, young adult, cult, fashionable fiction & non-fiction with a fierce twist.